IT'S GOING TO BE FABULOUS
THE COLORING BOOK

By Matthew E. Breer

An adult coloring book, inspired by diamonds, gems, all things Fabulous, and shiny!

Over 40 illustrations for hours of stress relieving fun!

This book makes a perfect gift for everyone!

I0432748

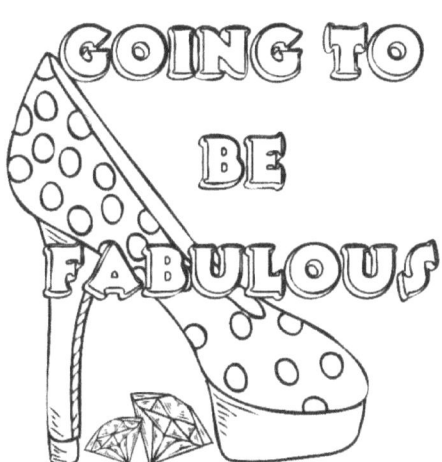

Be sure to check us out on Facebook and our website for other great things!

http://breerspublishing.weebly.com/

https://www.facebook.com/BreersPublishing/

Images in this book are created from public domain creative commons, royalty – free vintage art, and original art work. Copyright 2016 Breer's Art & Things Vintage publishing. All rights reserved.

IT'S GOING TO BE FABULOUS

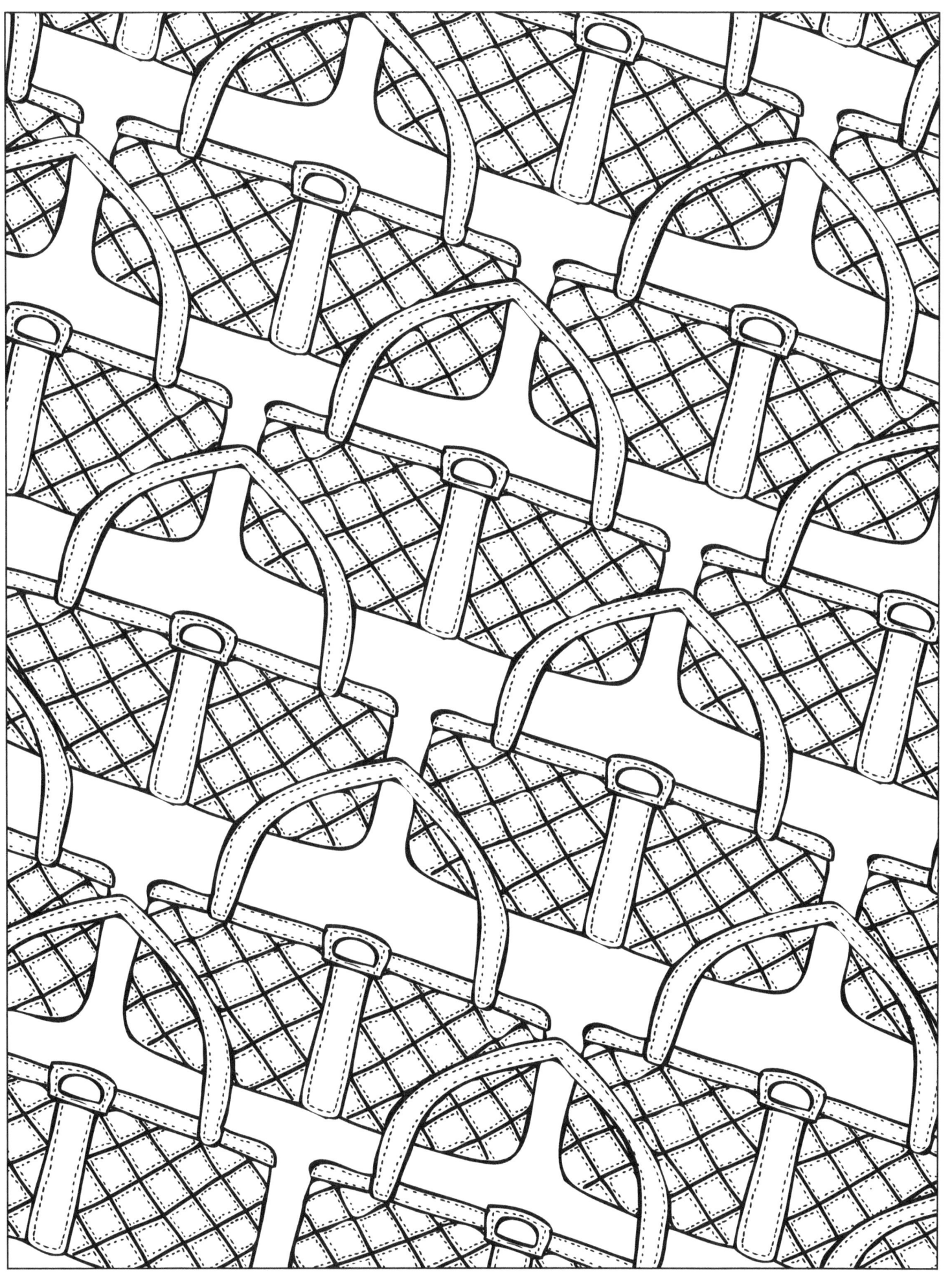

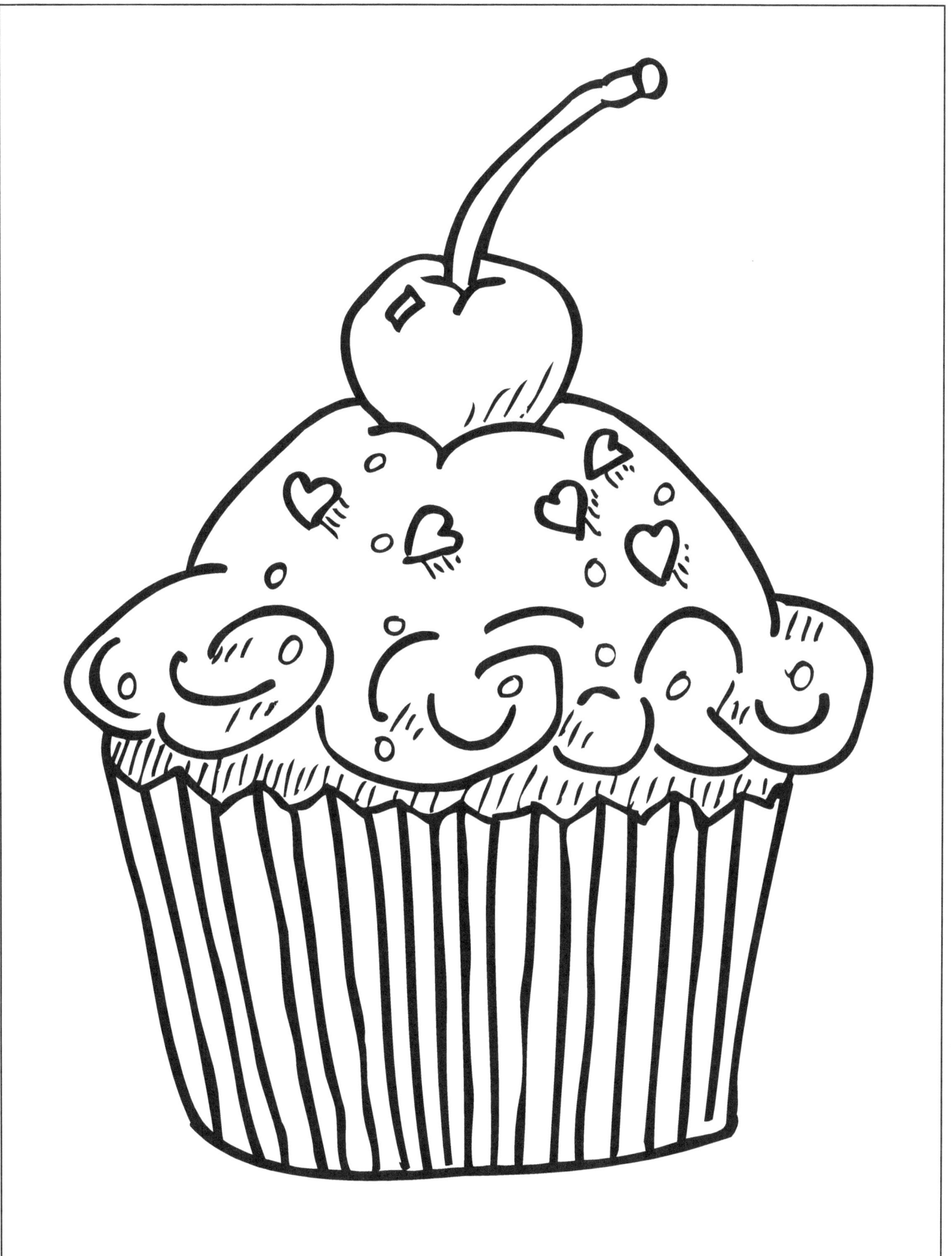

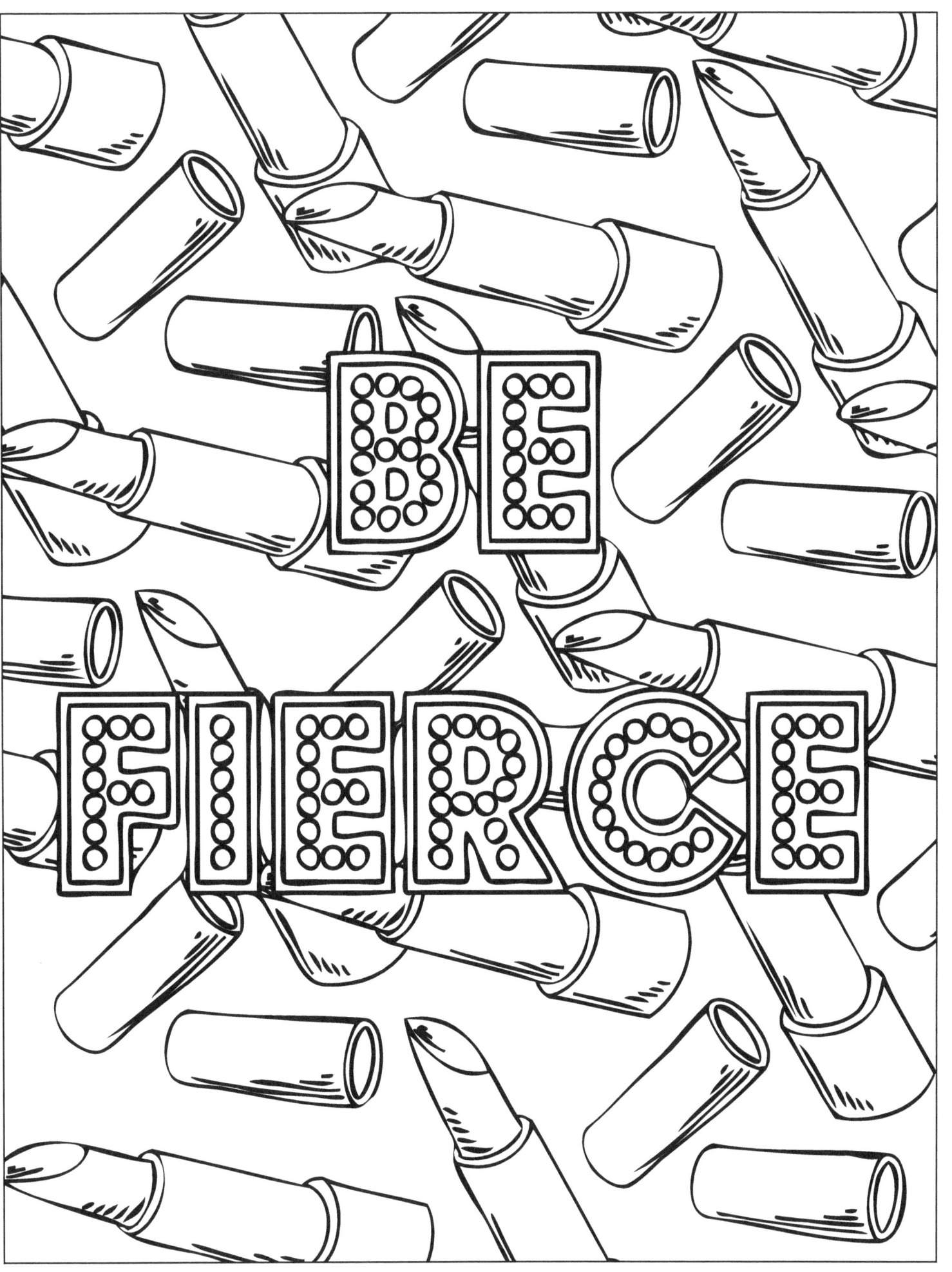

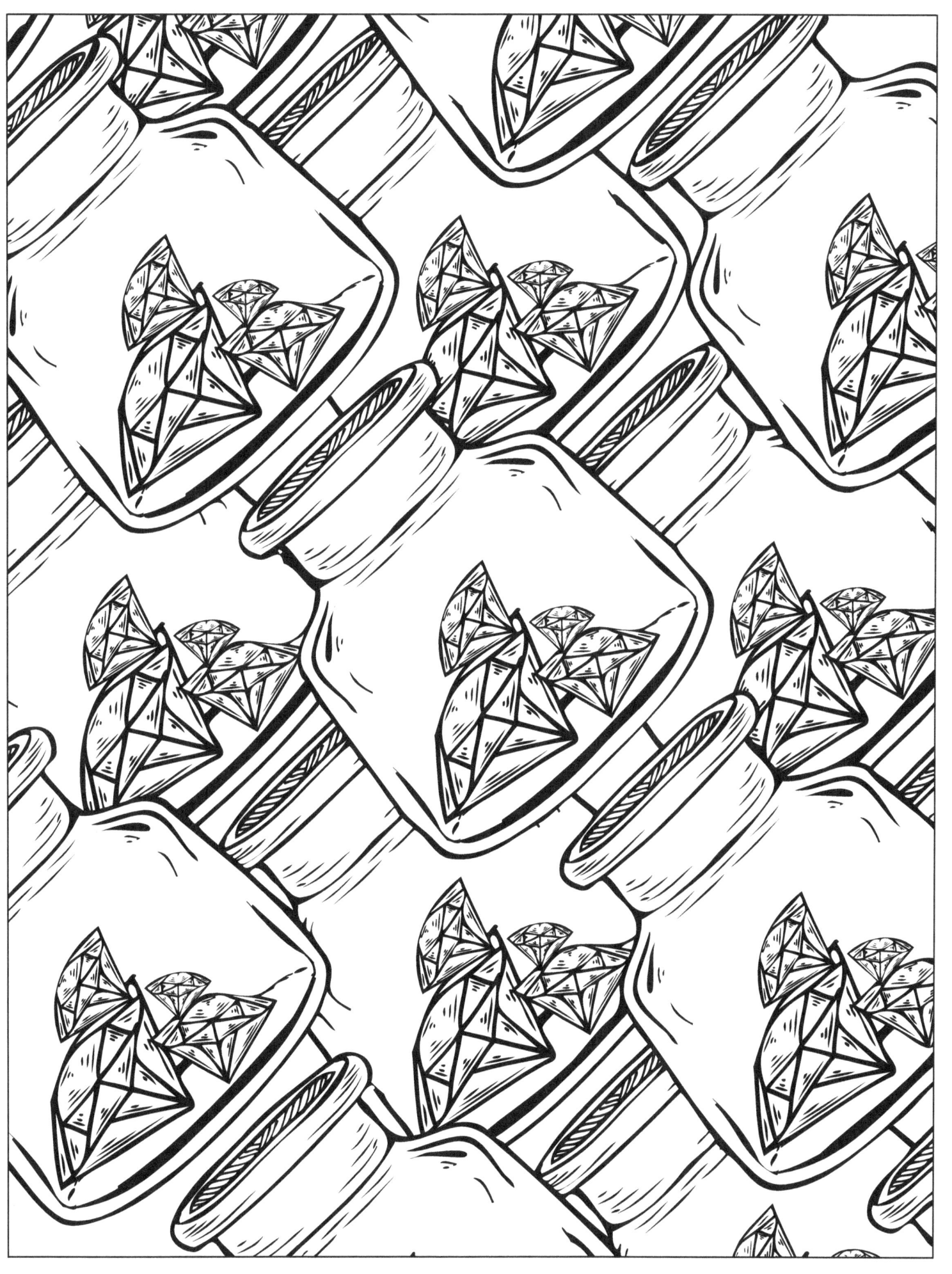

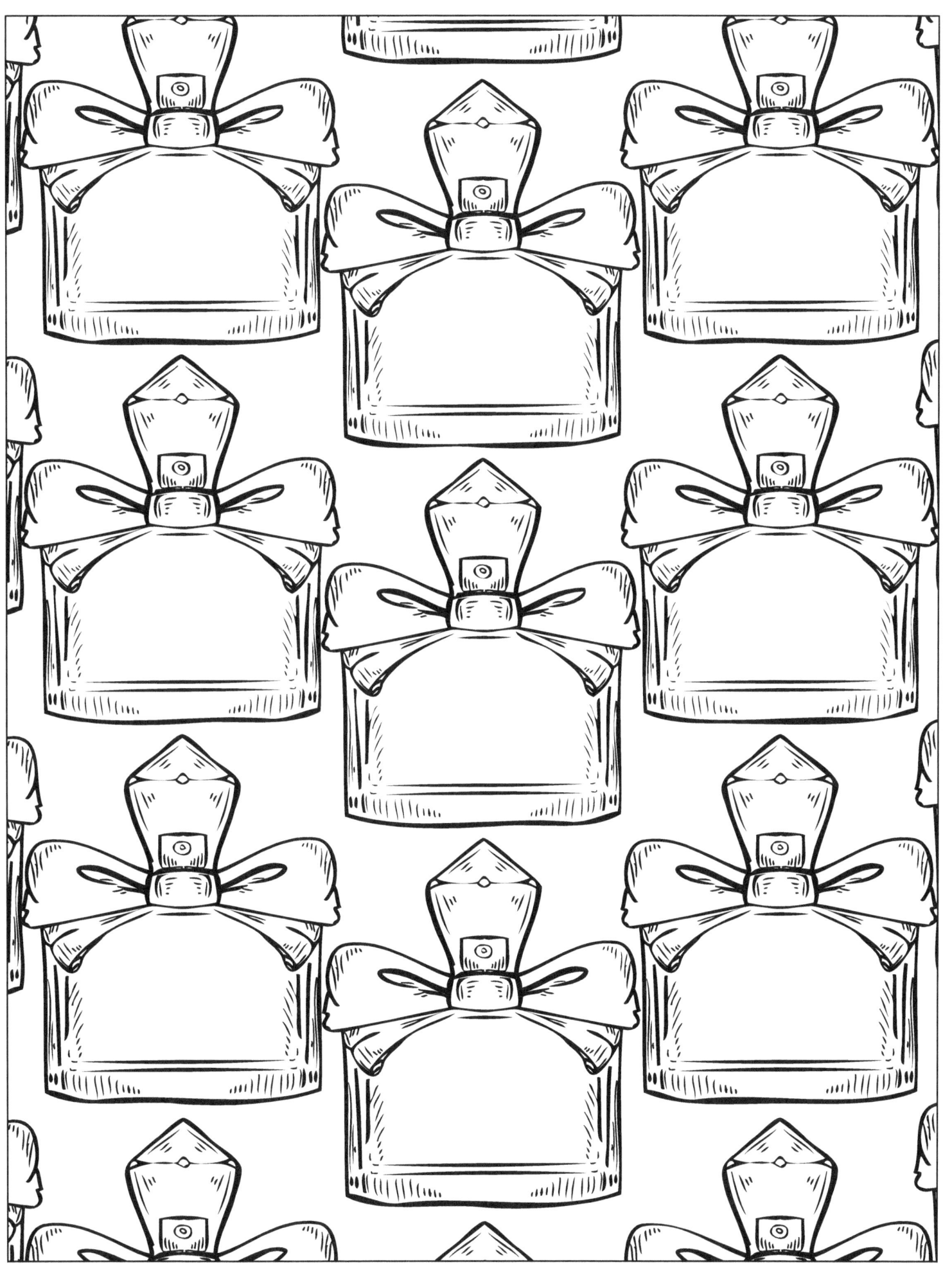

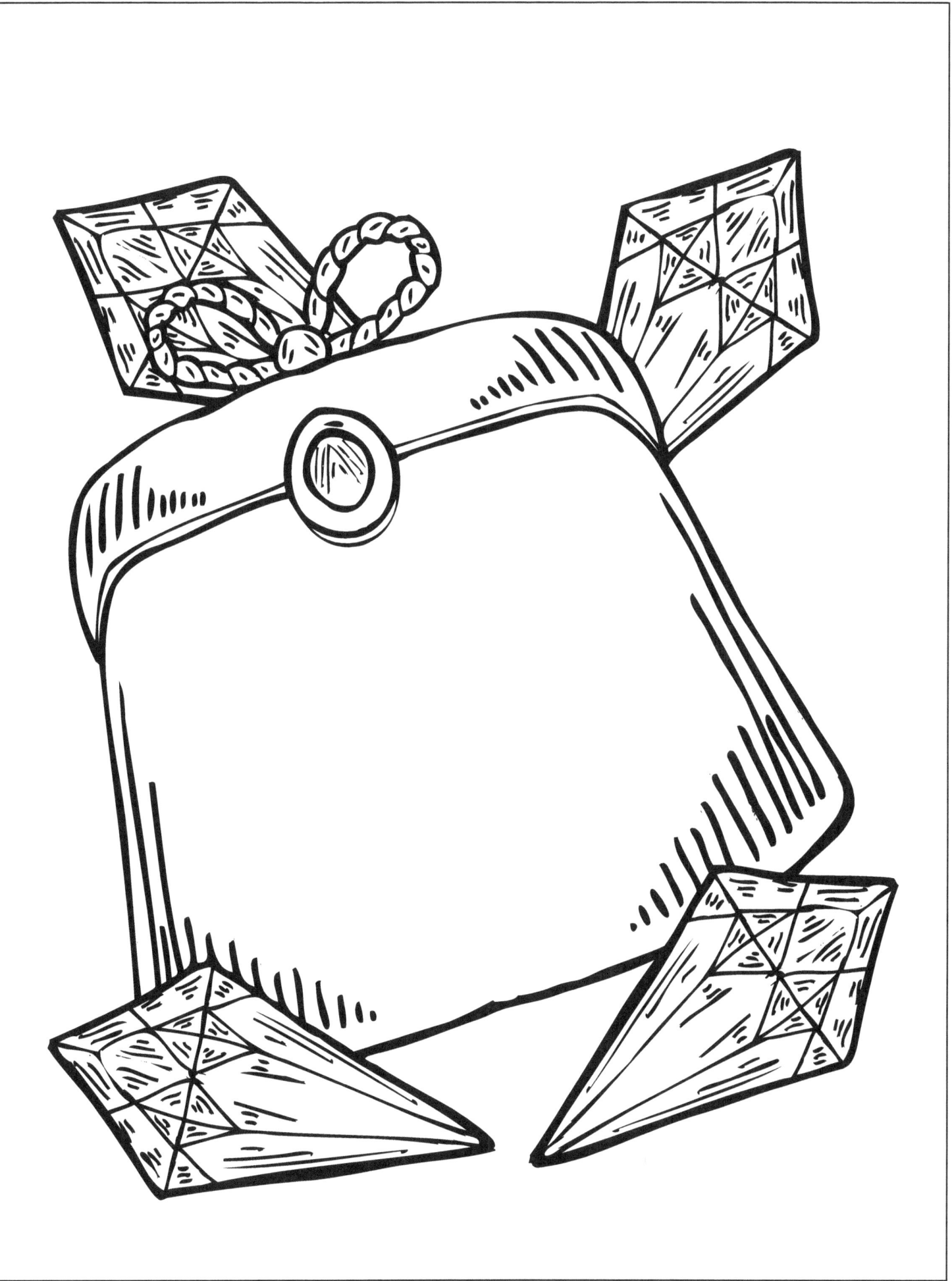

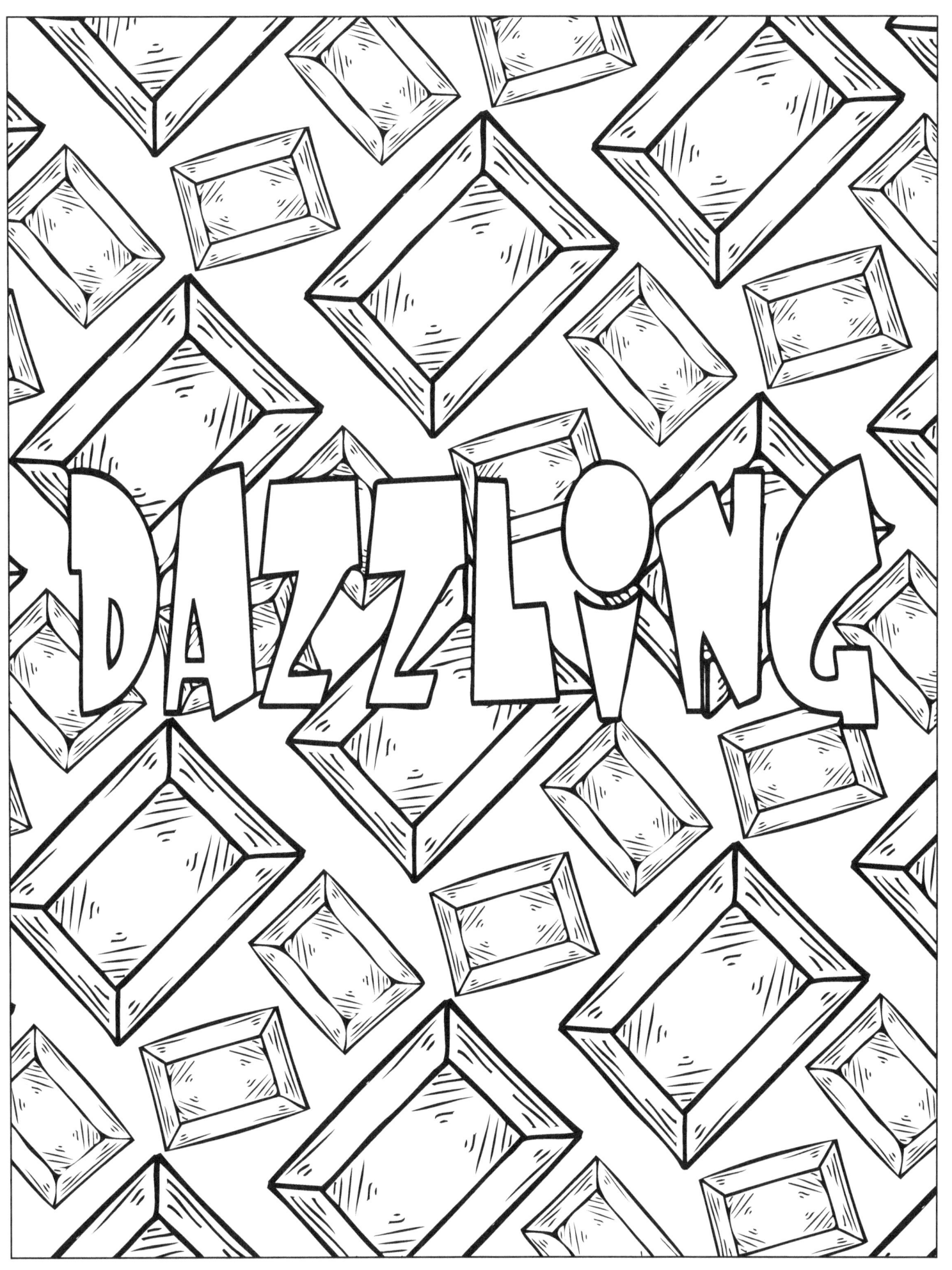

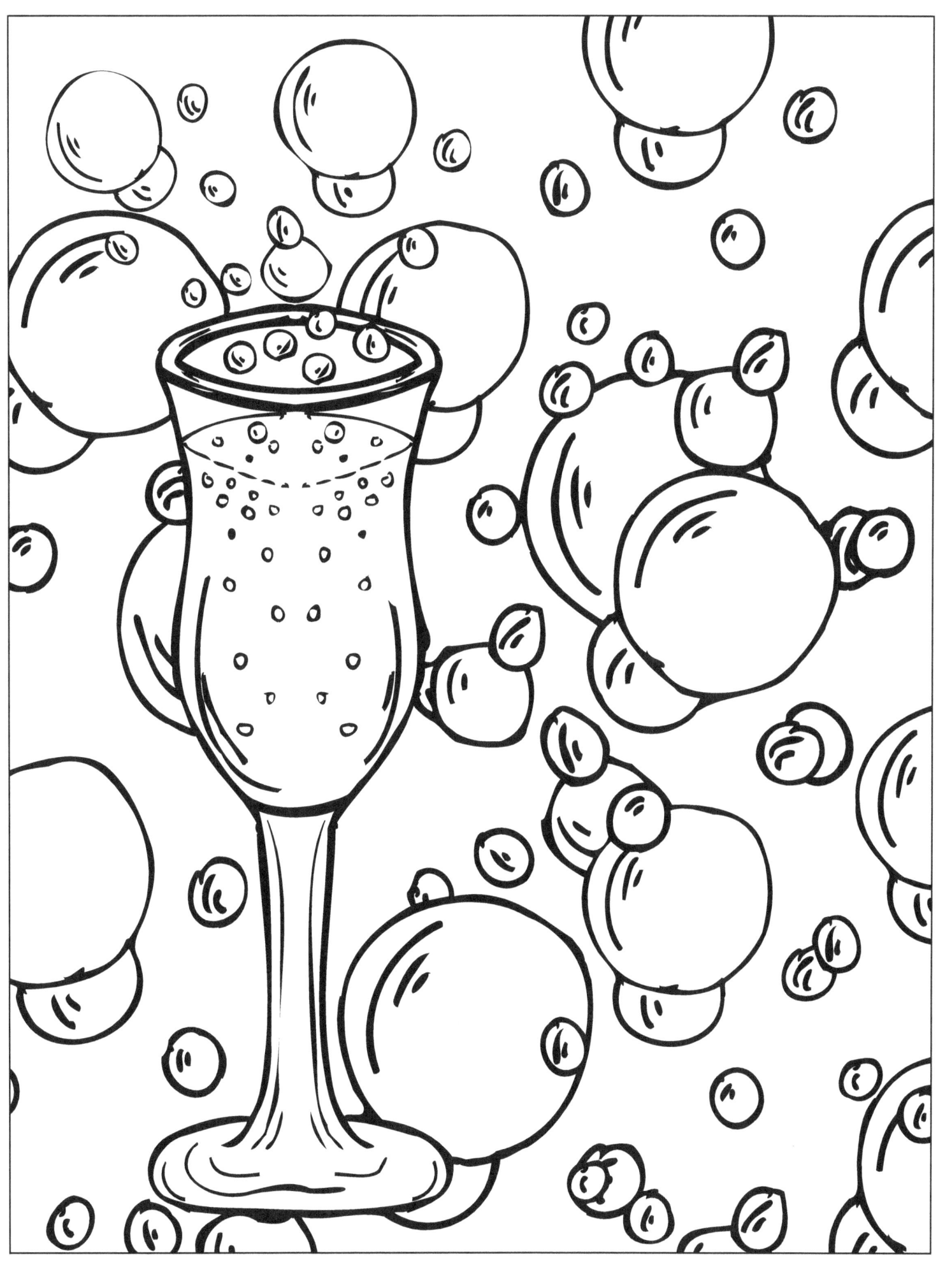

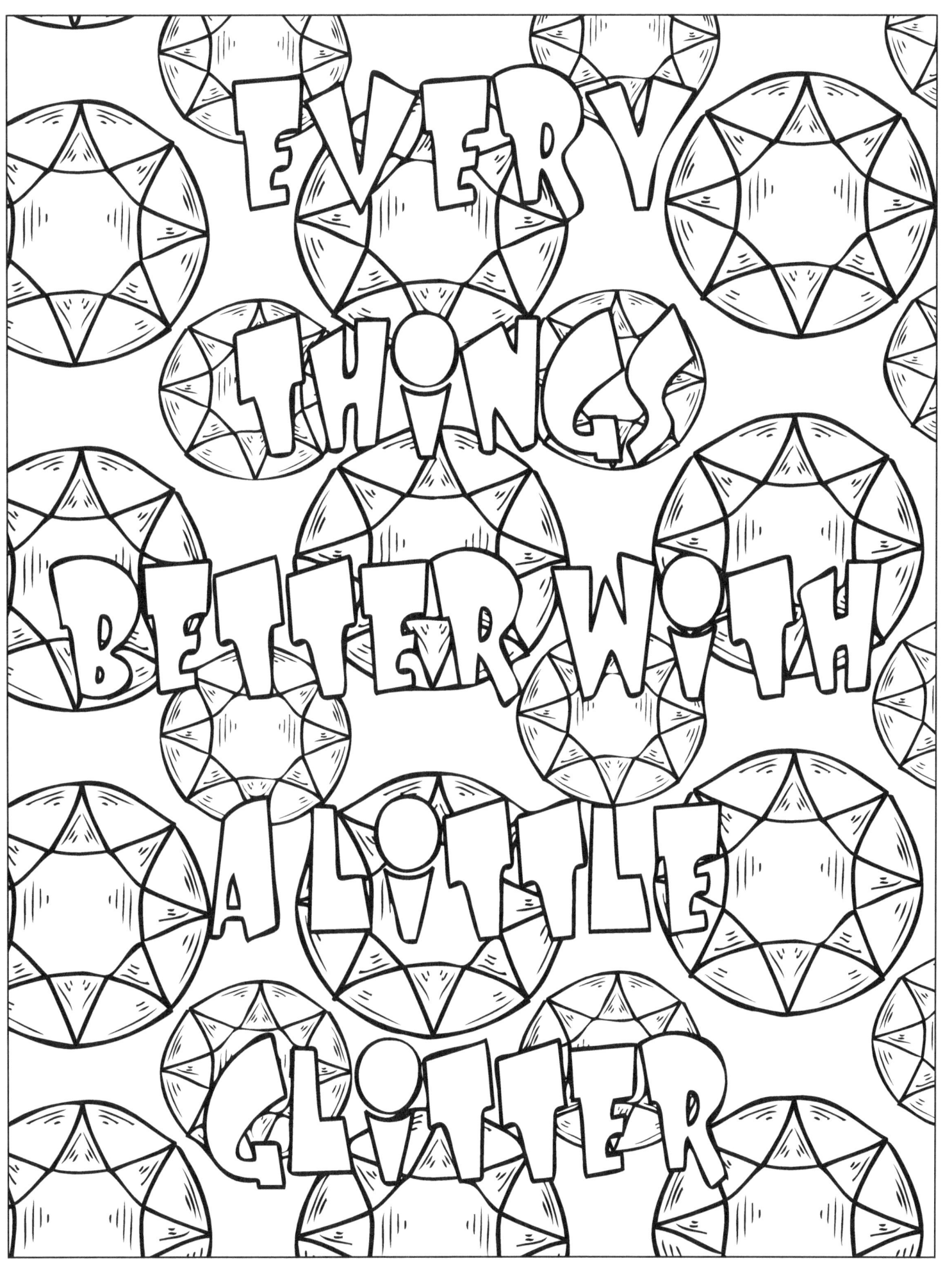

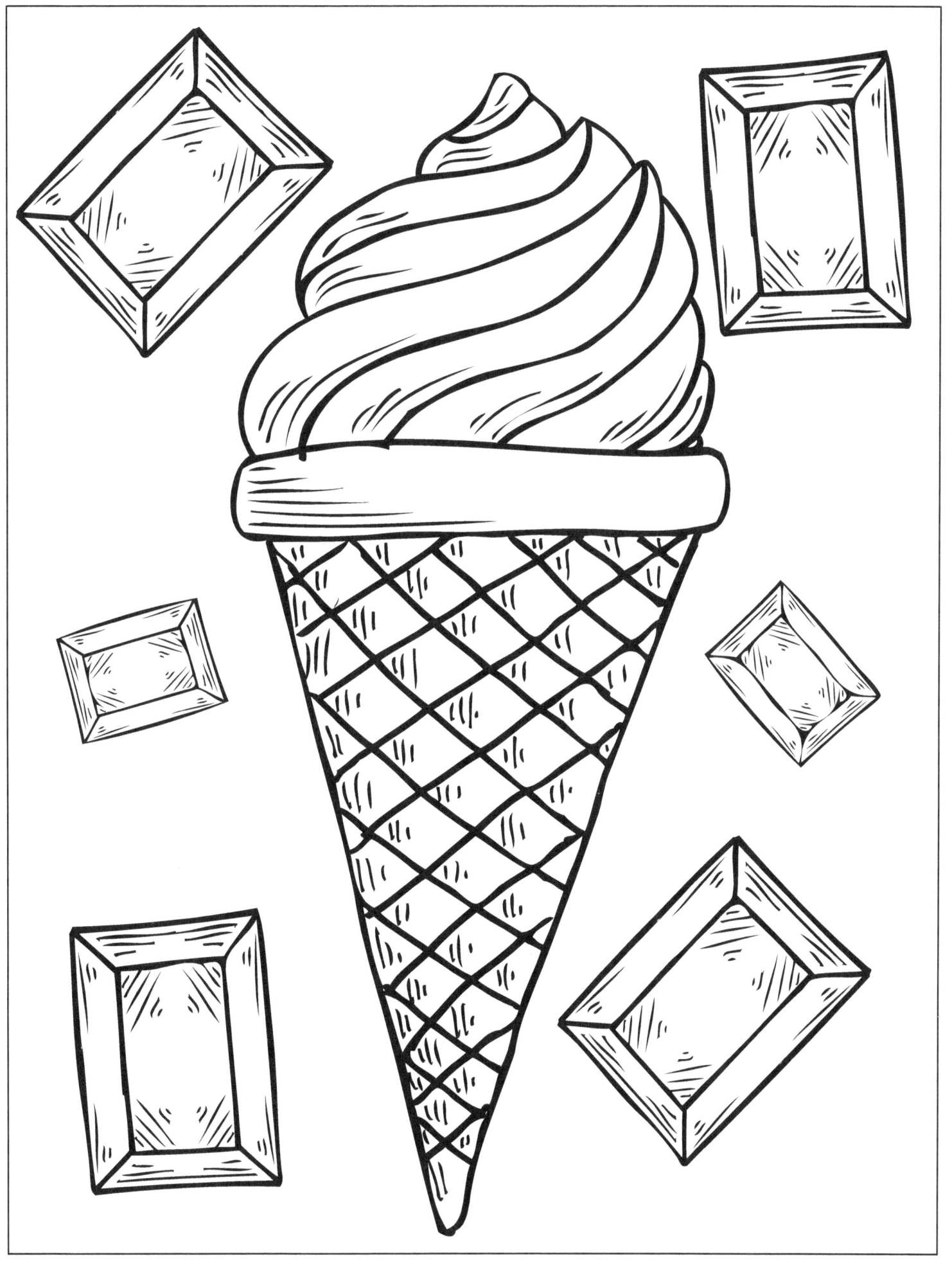

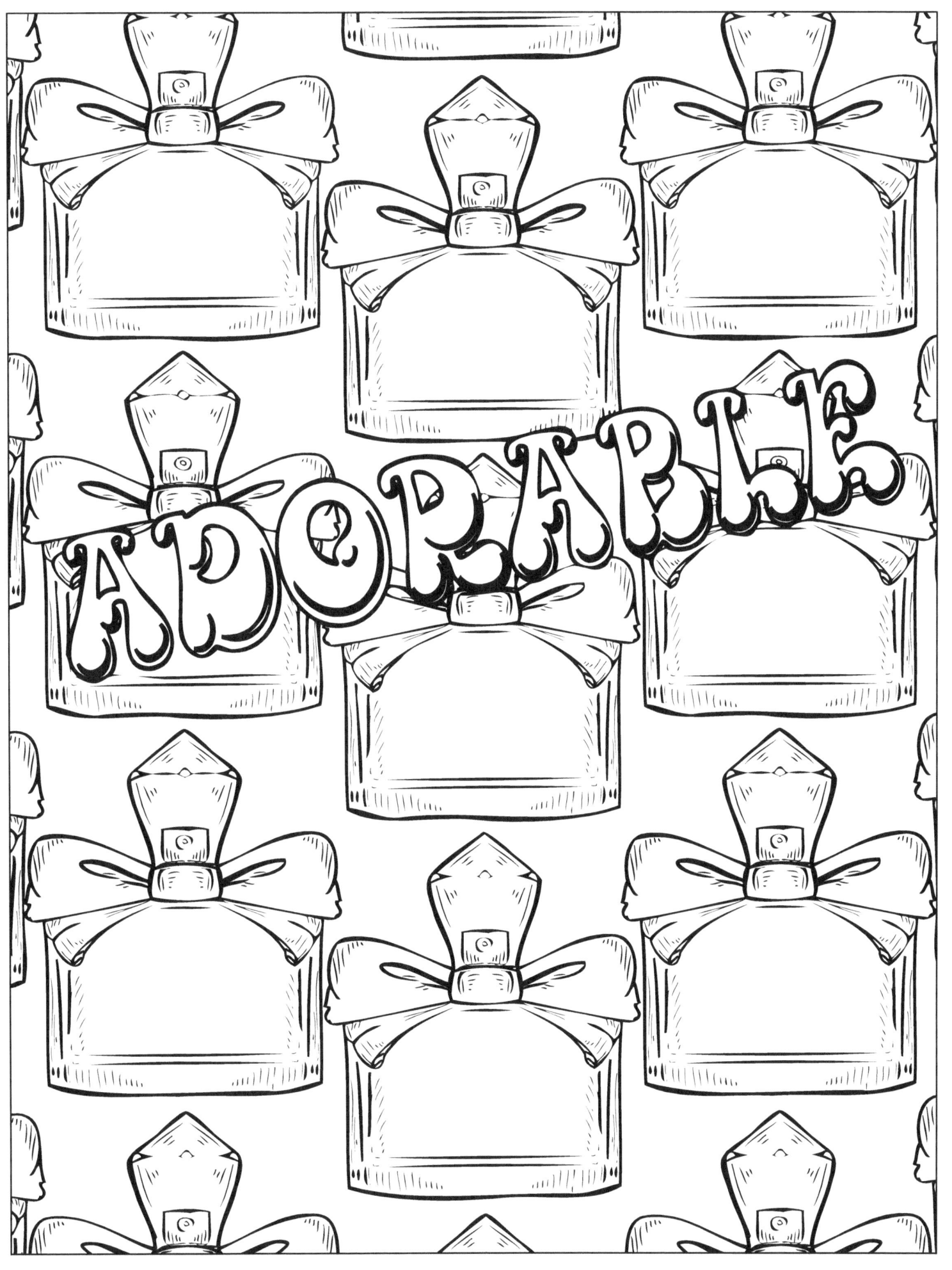

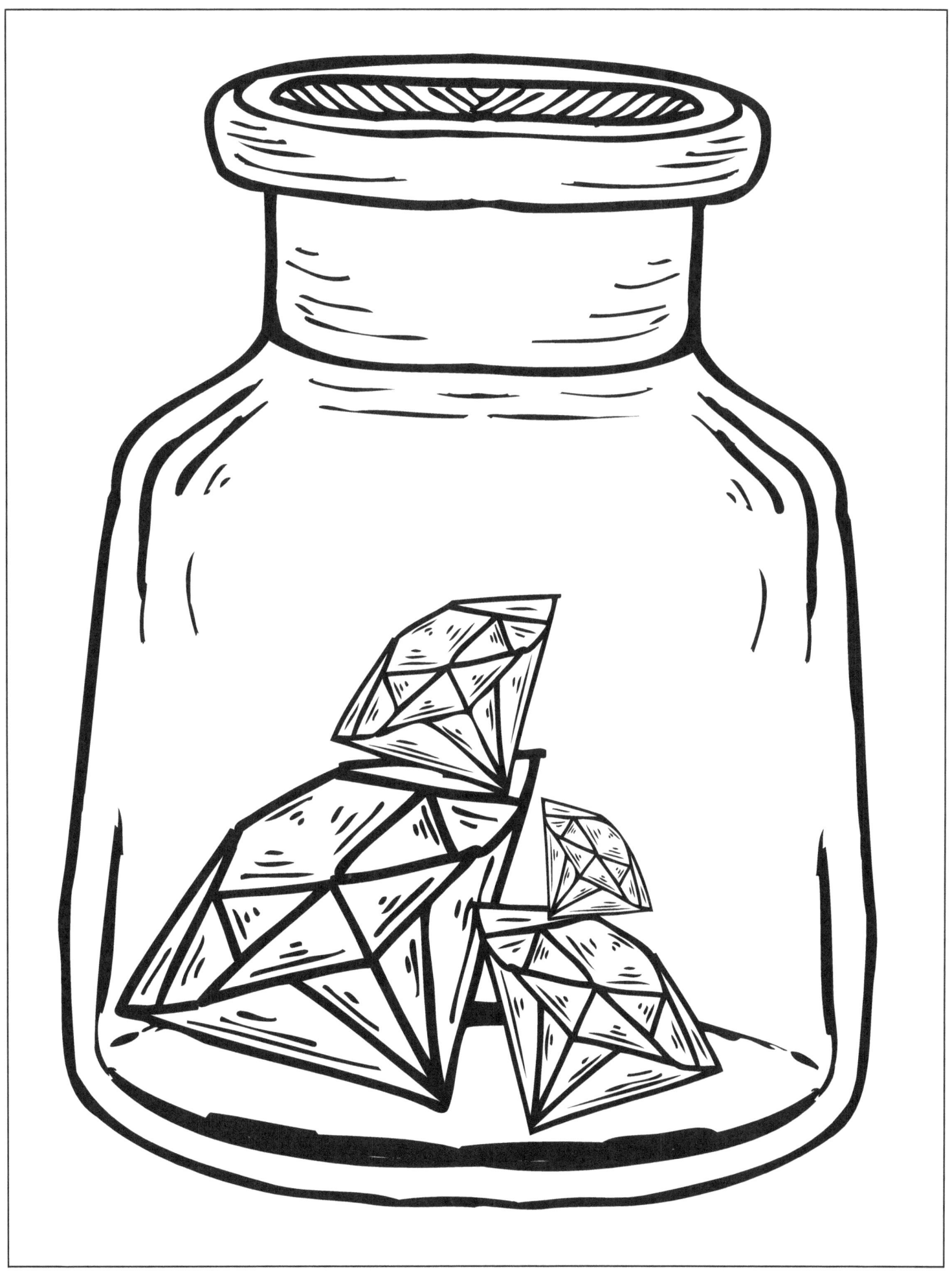

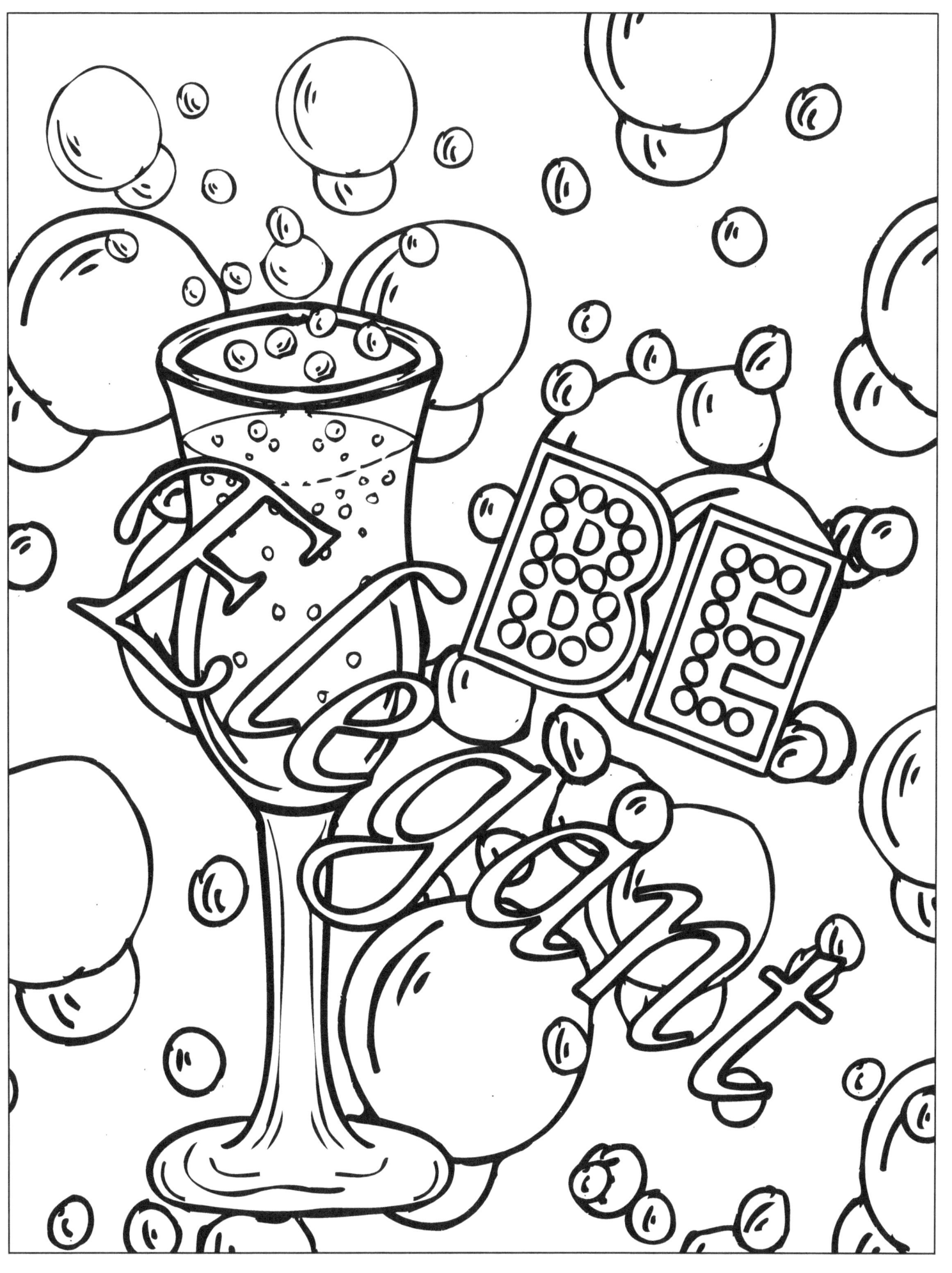

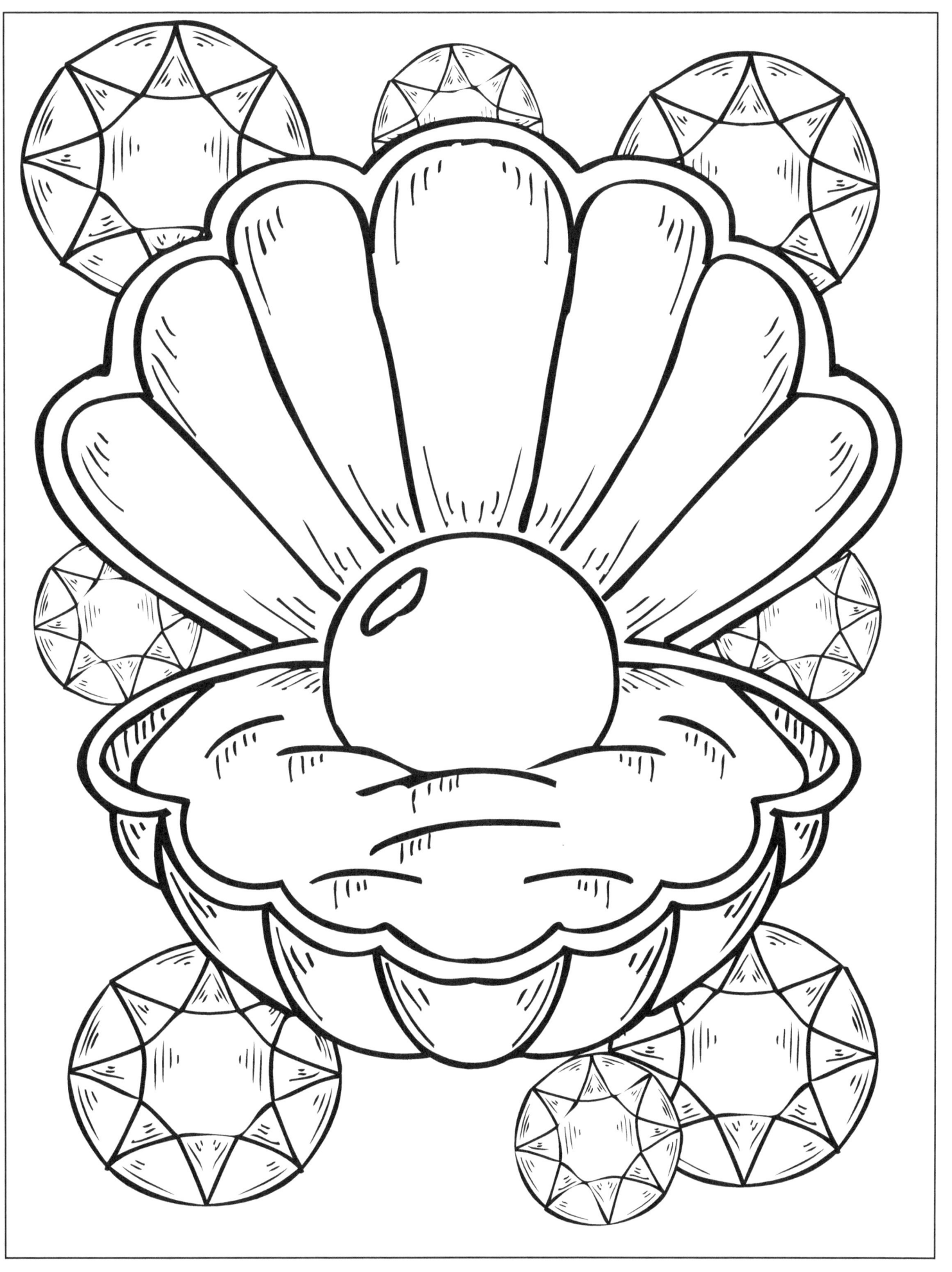

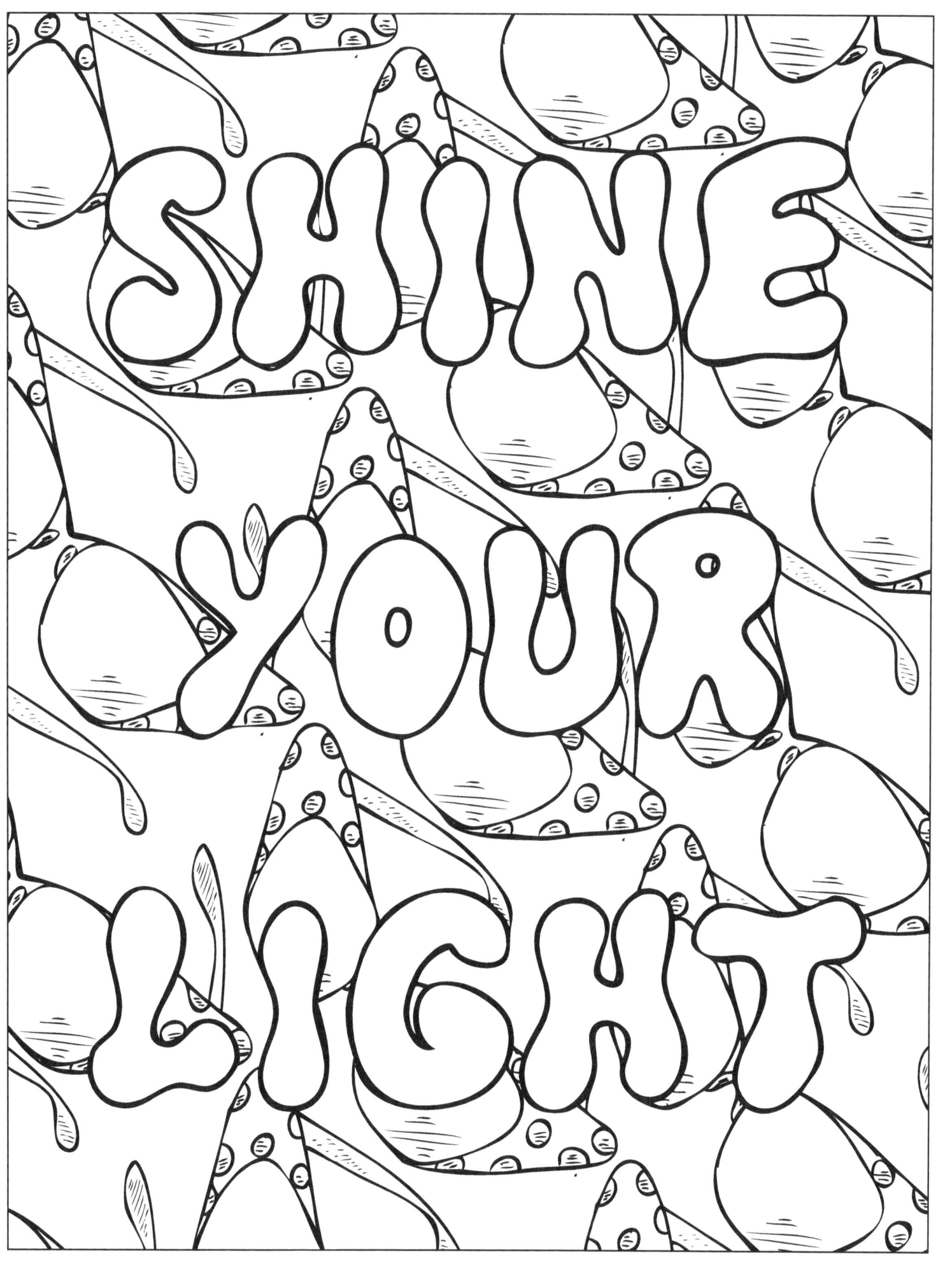

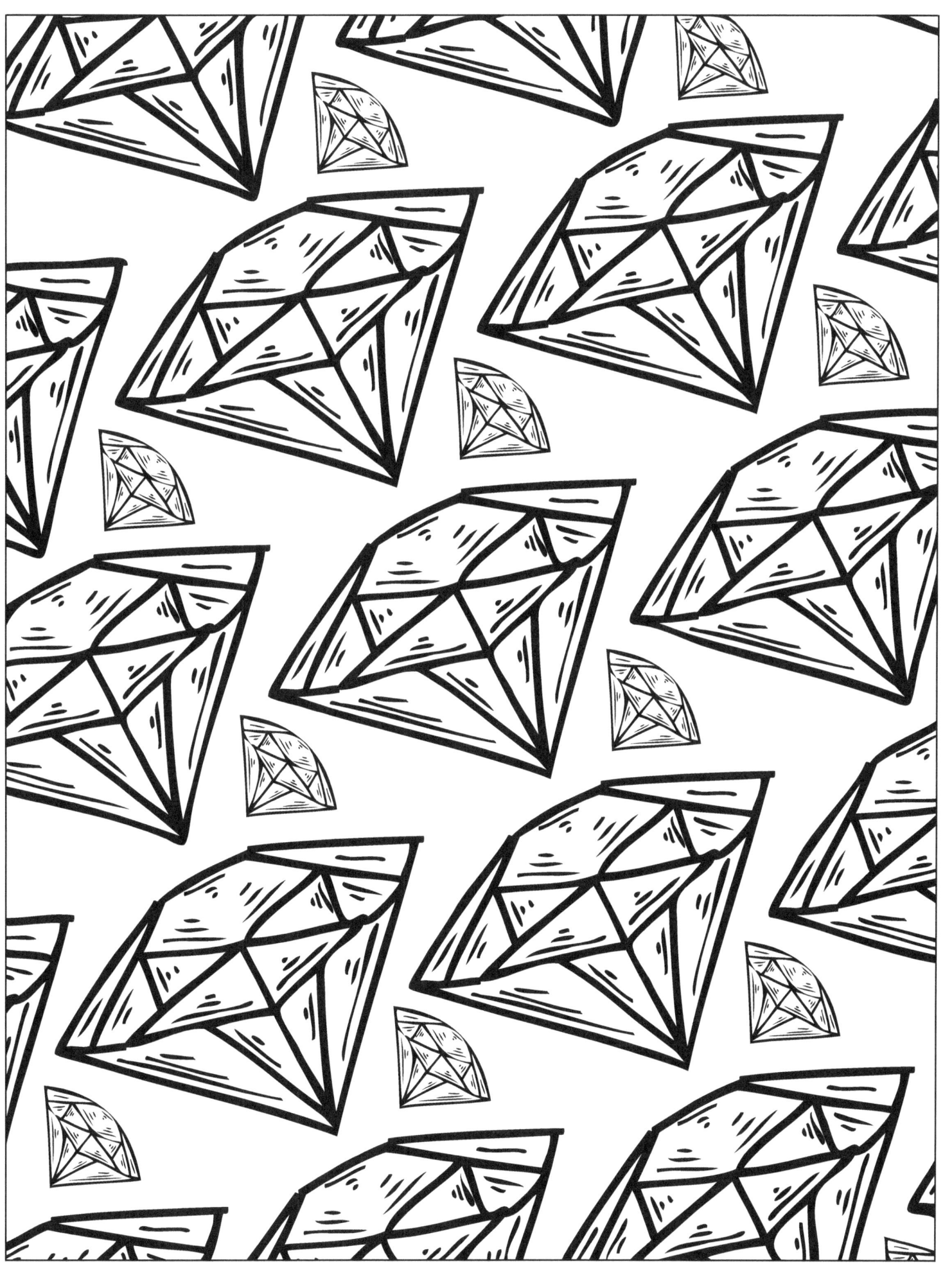

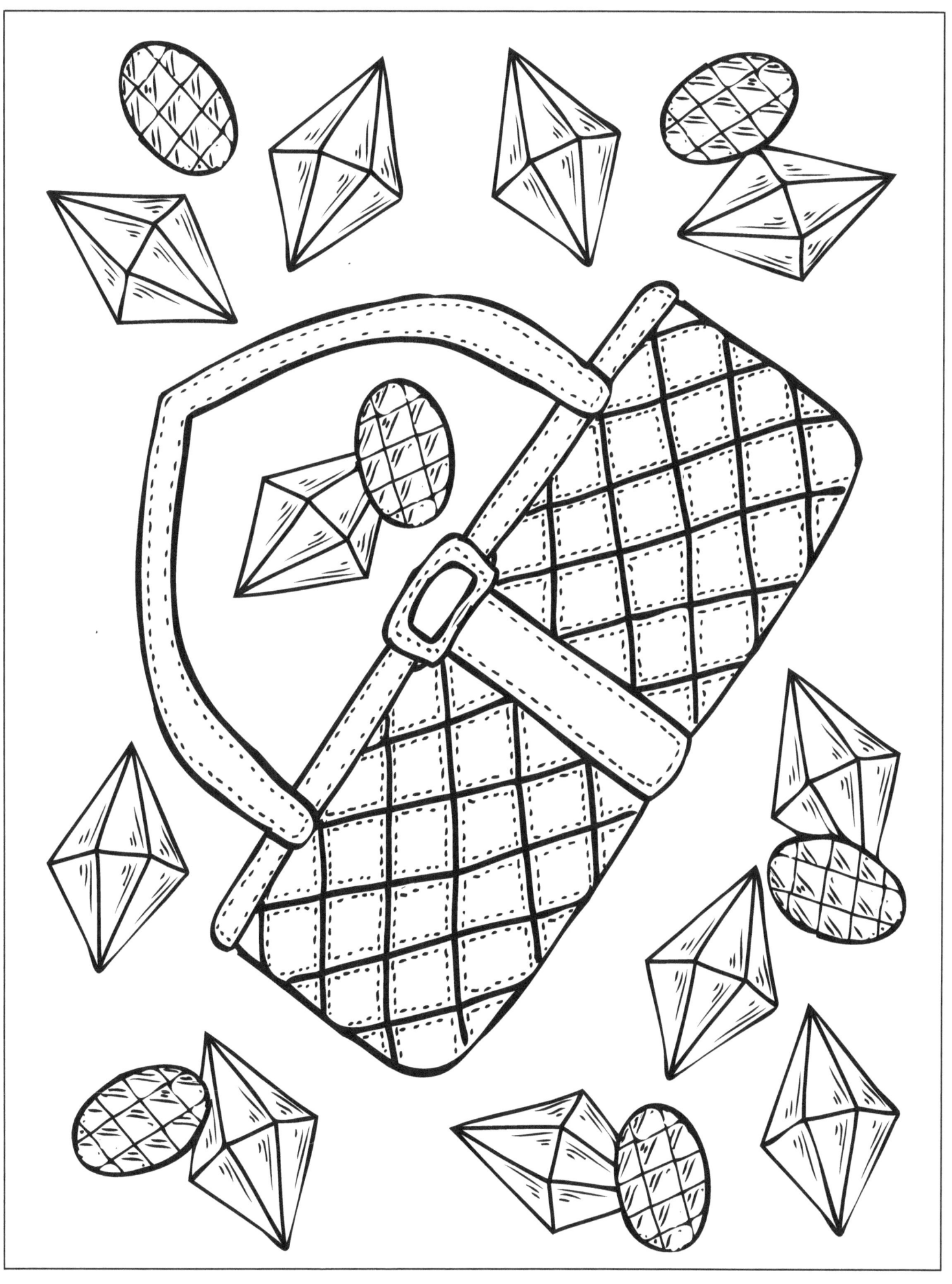

MY WORLD IS BRIGHTER BECAUSE OF YOU

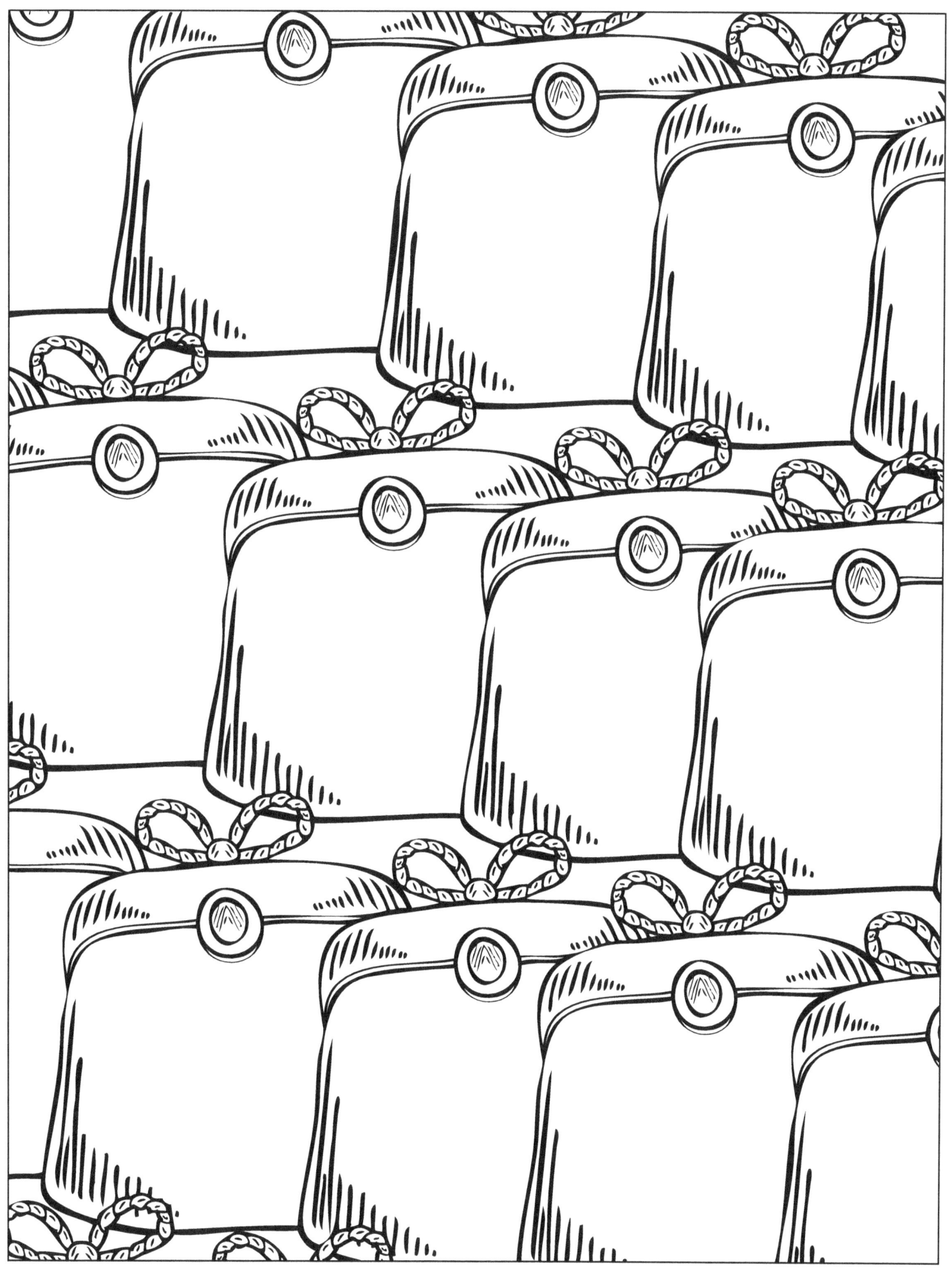

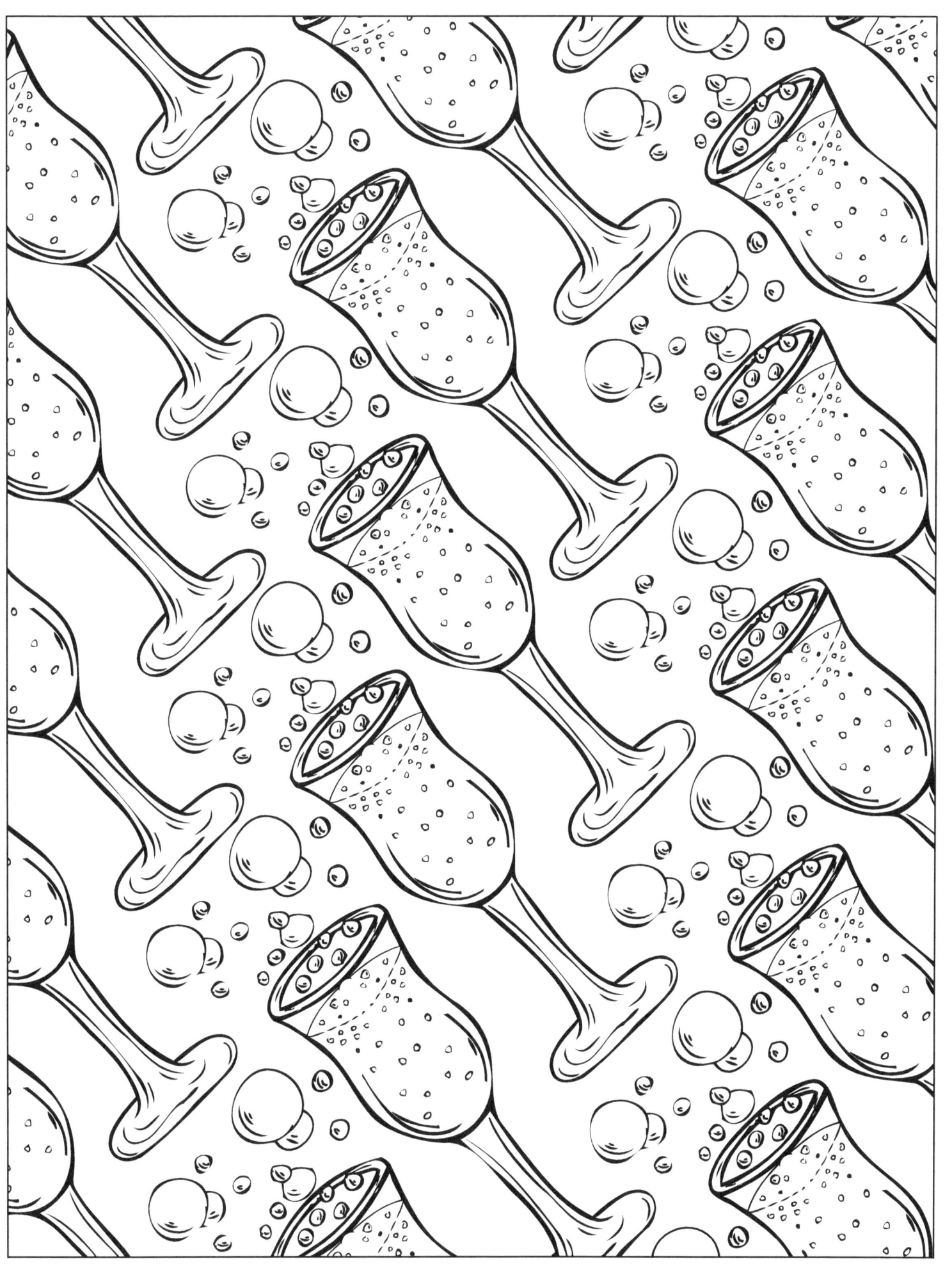

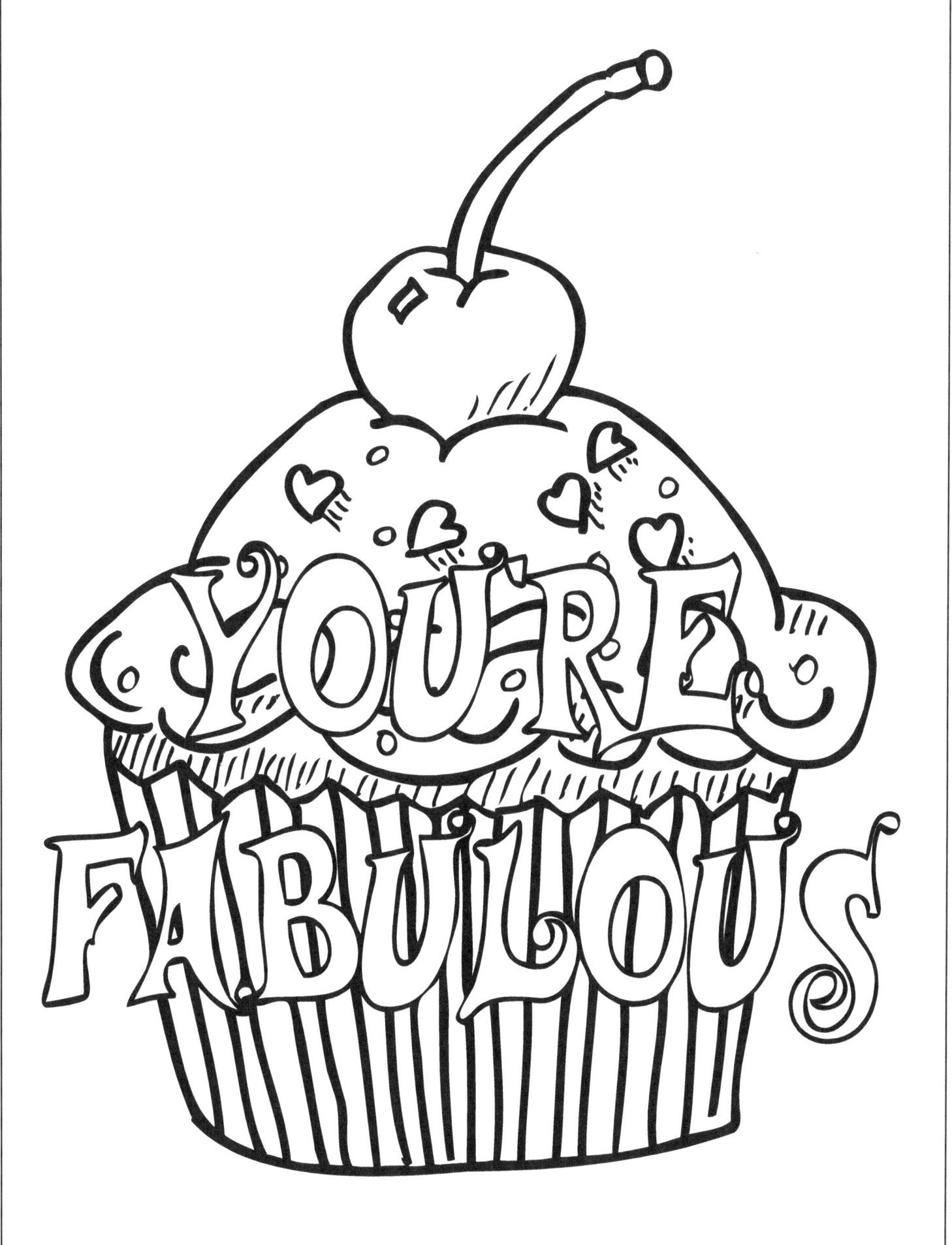

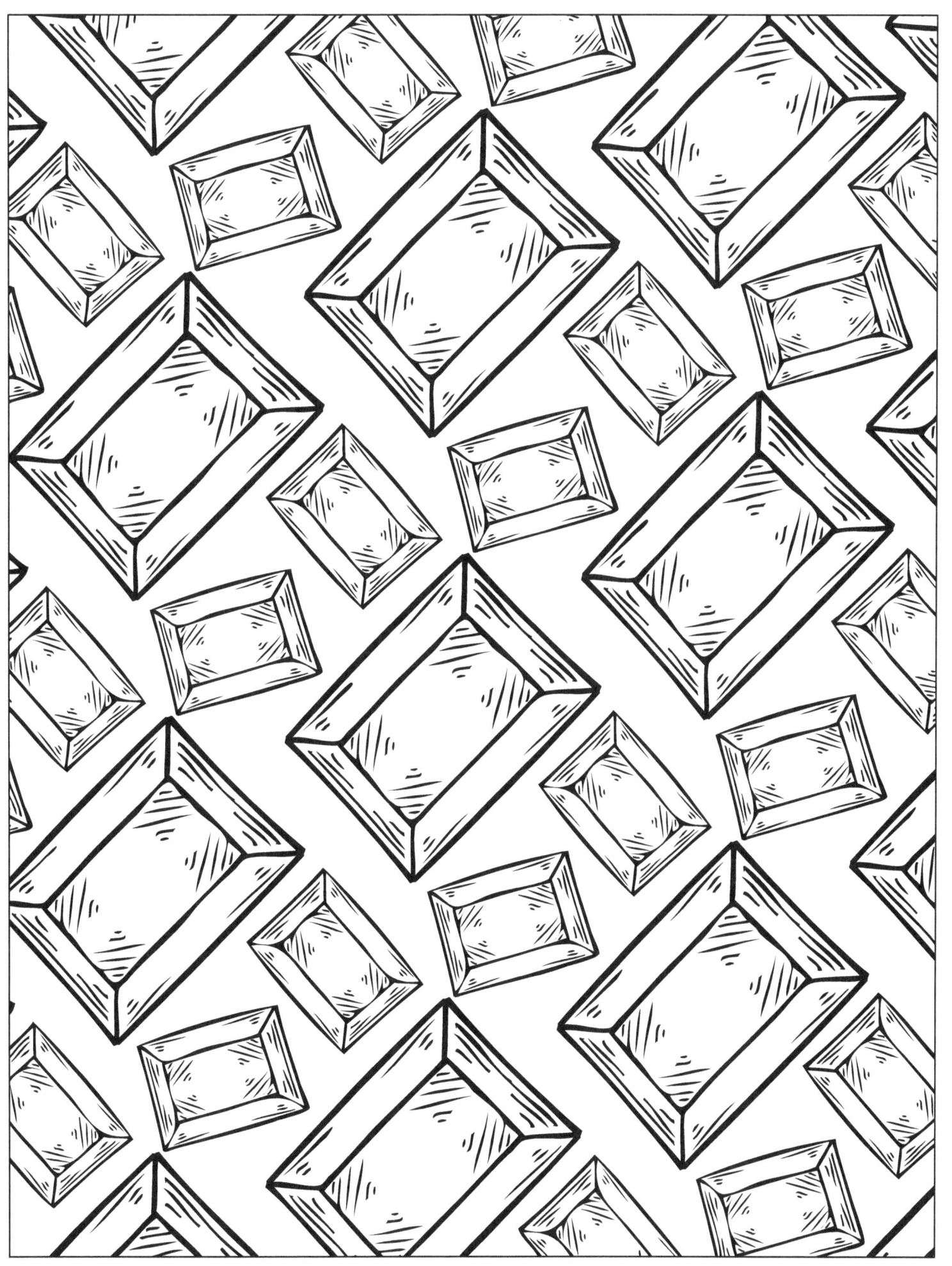

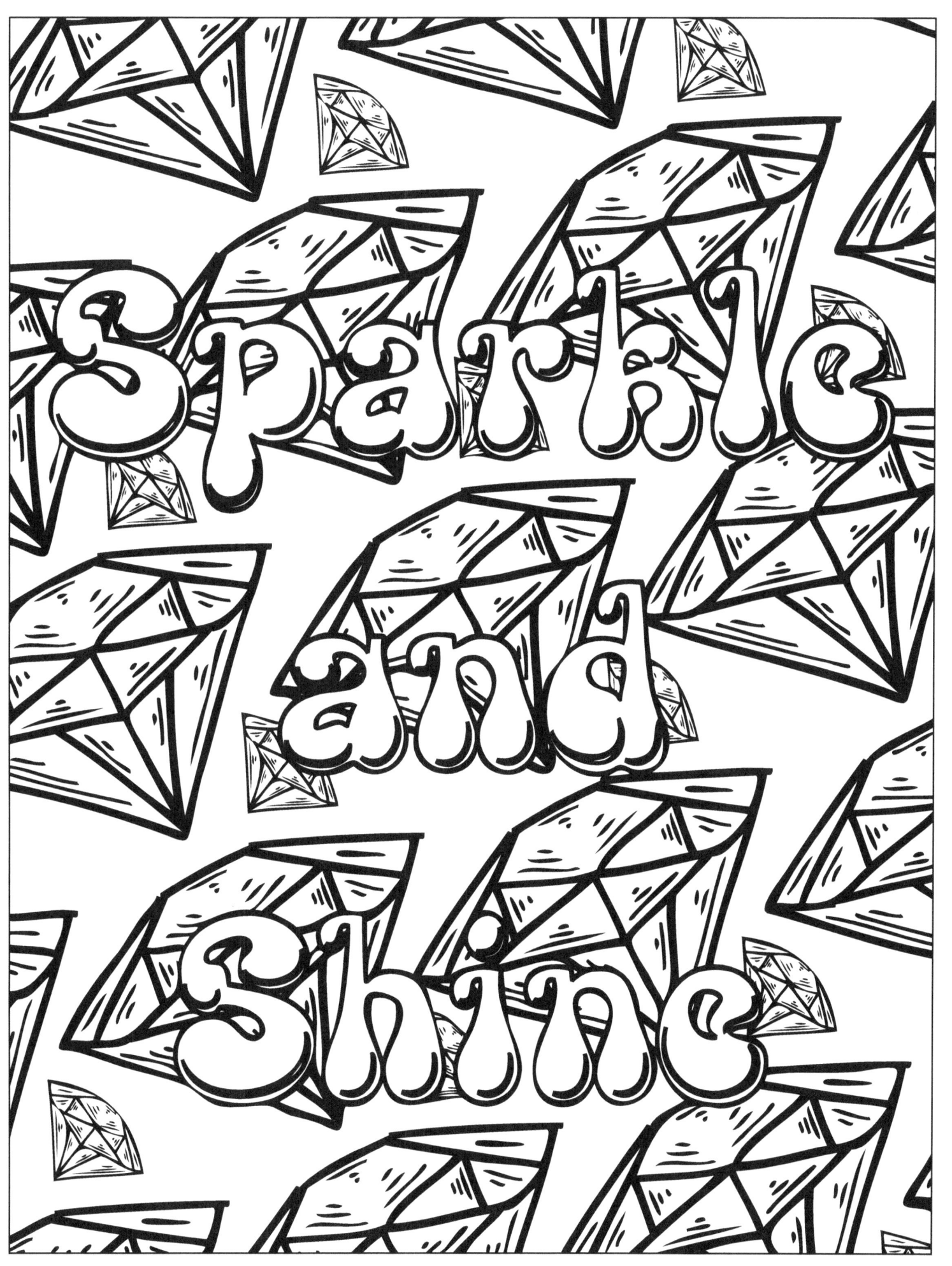

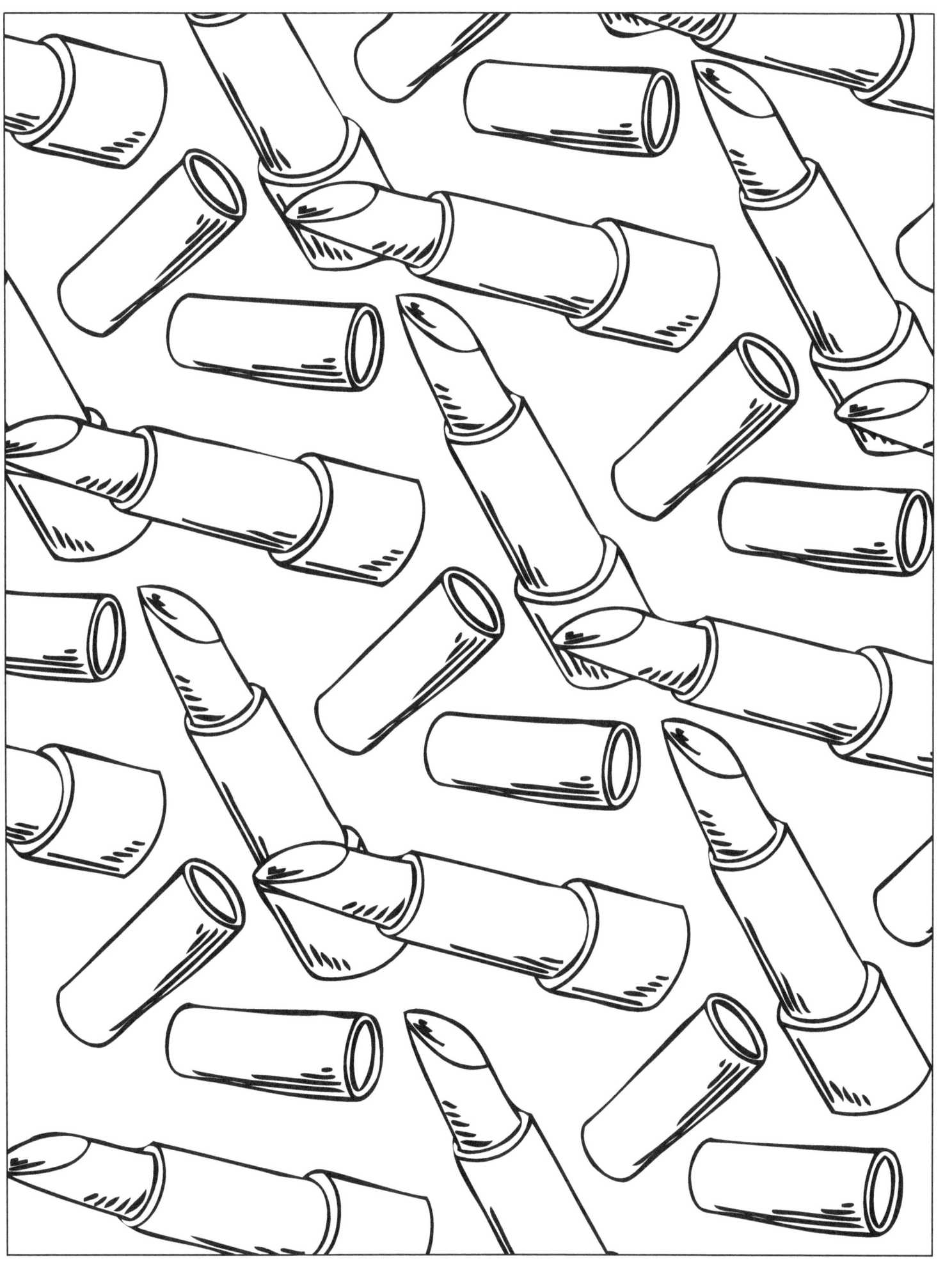

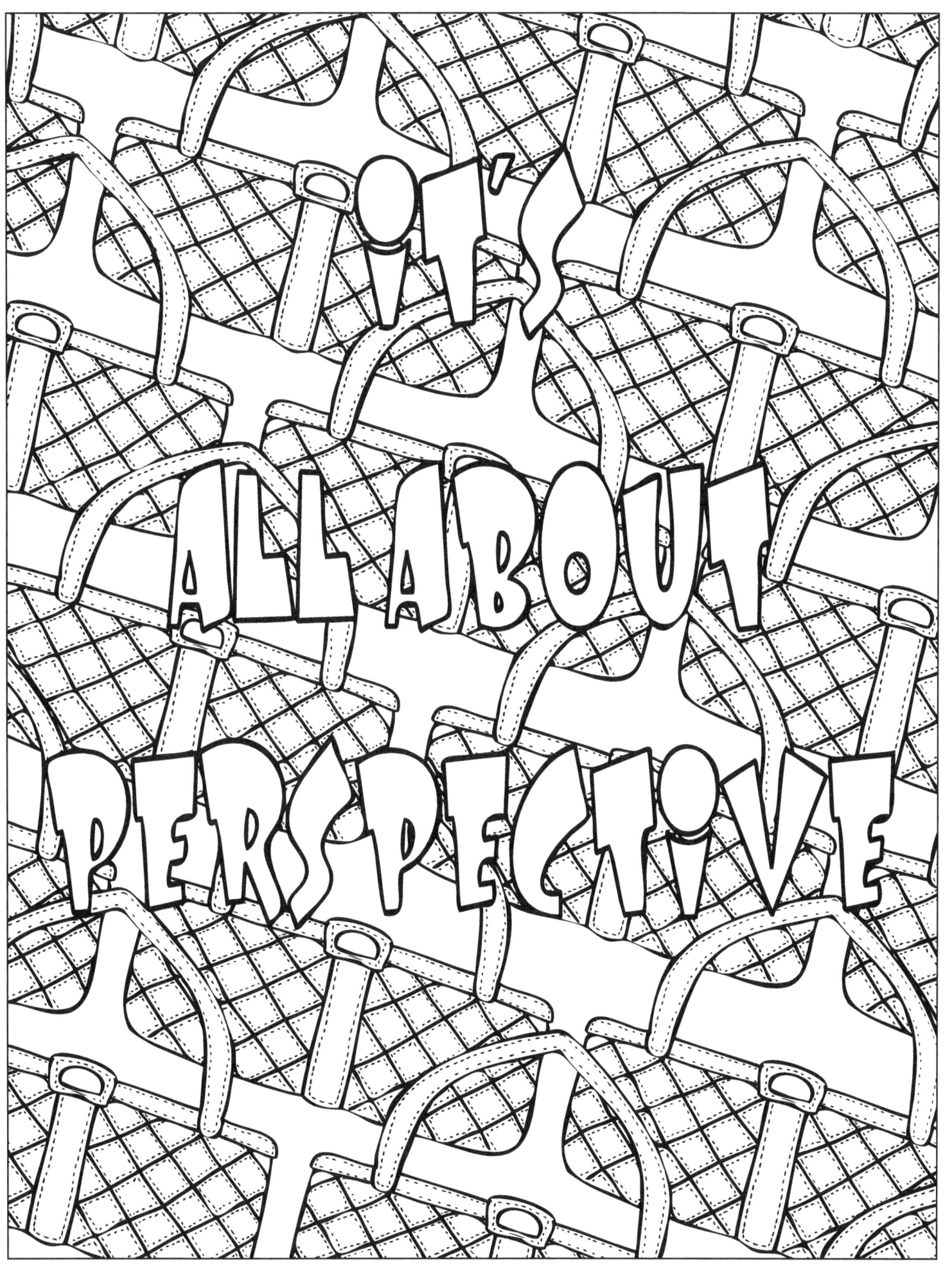

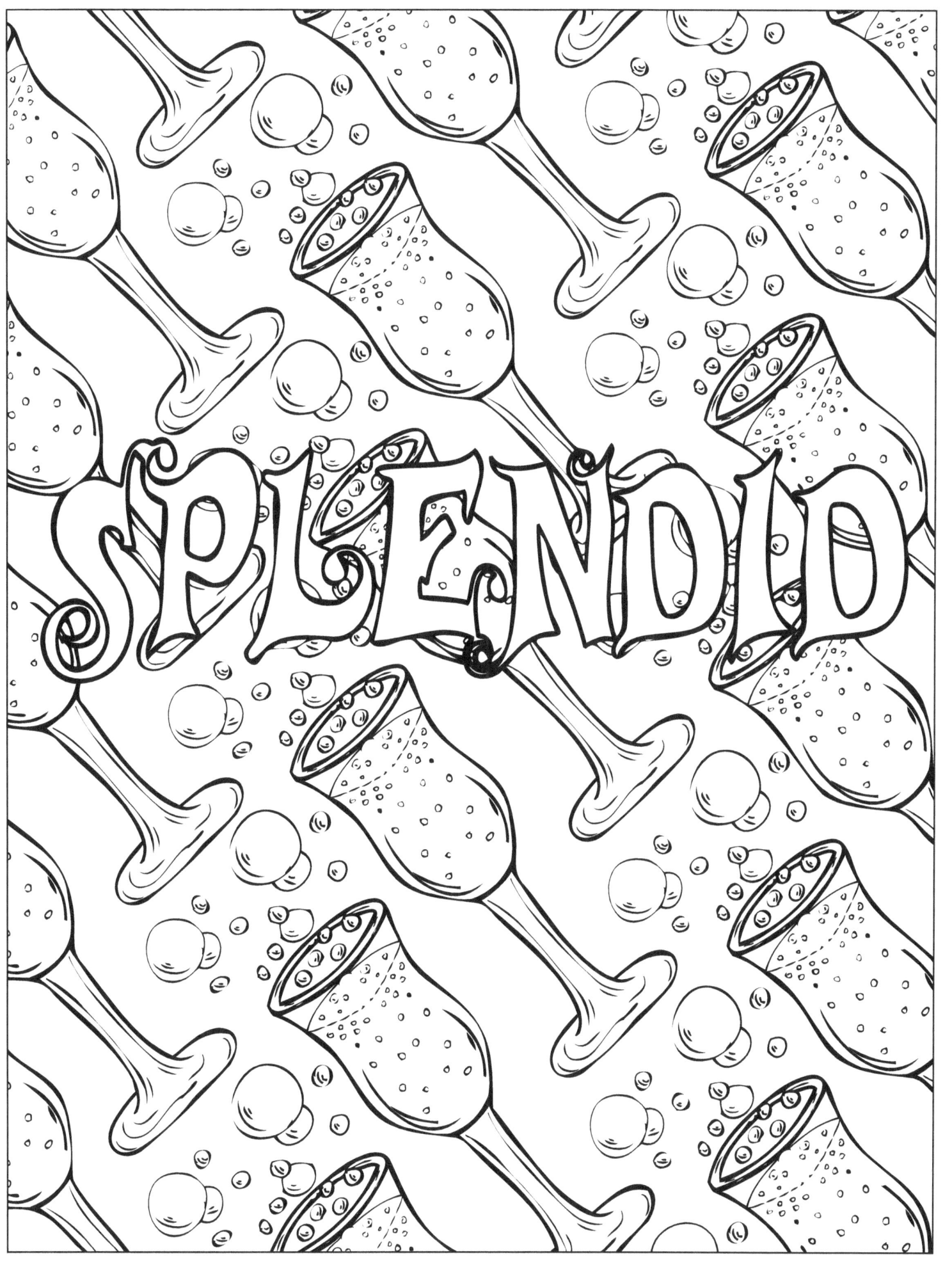

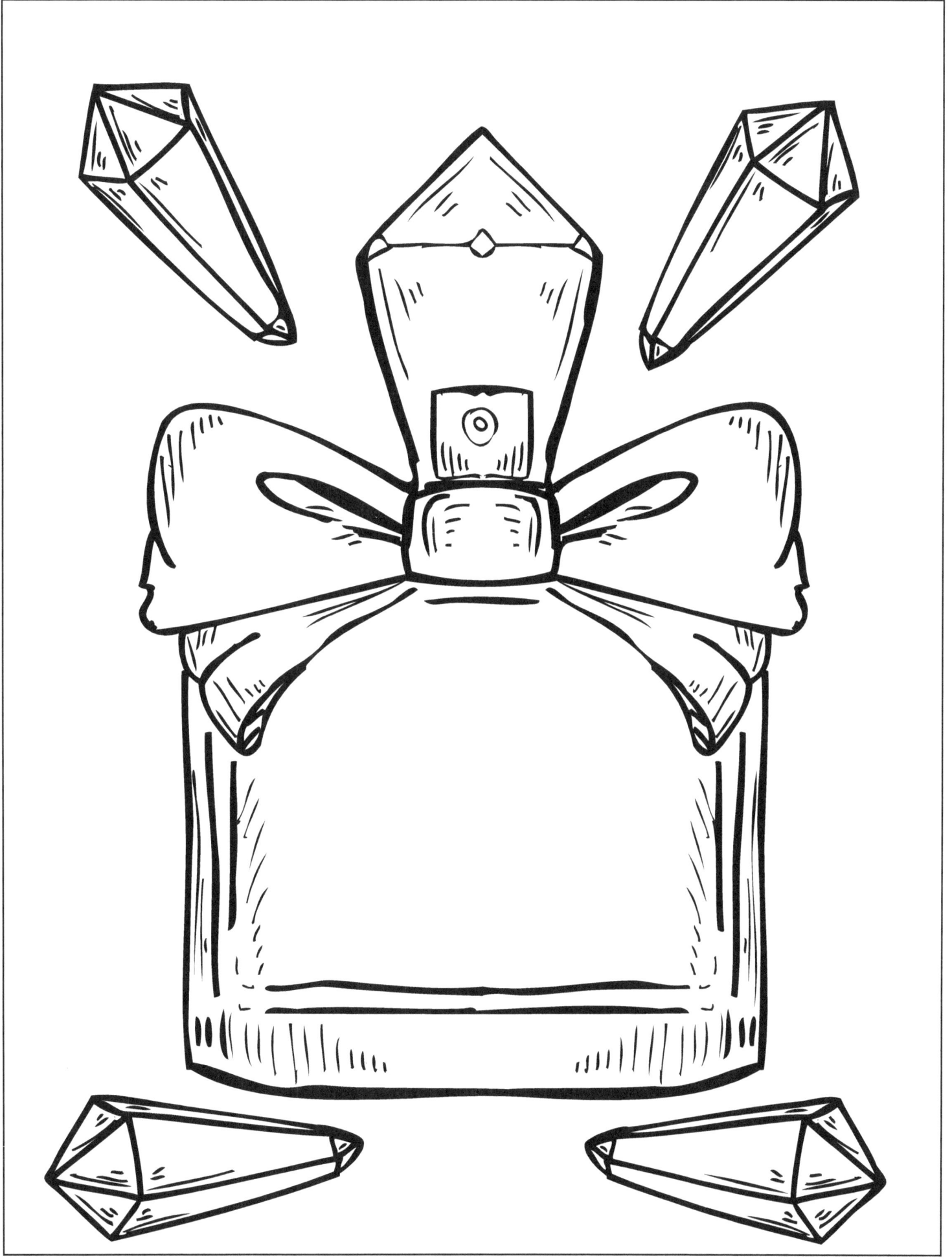

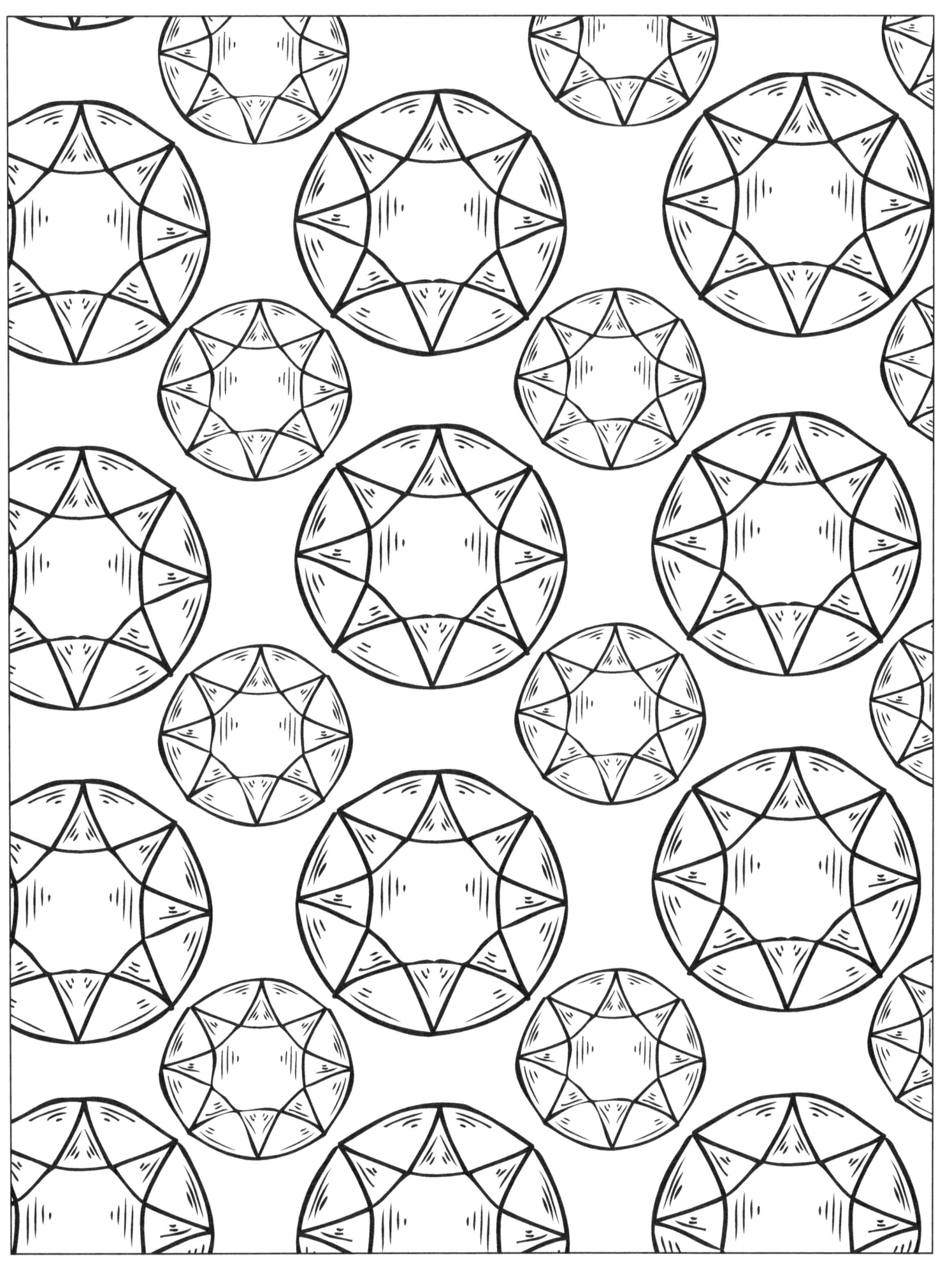

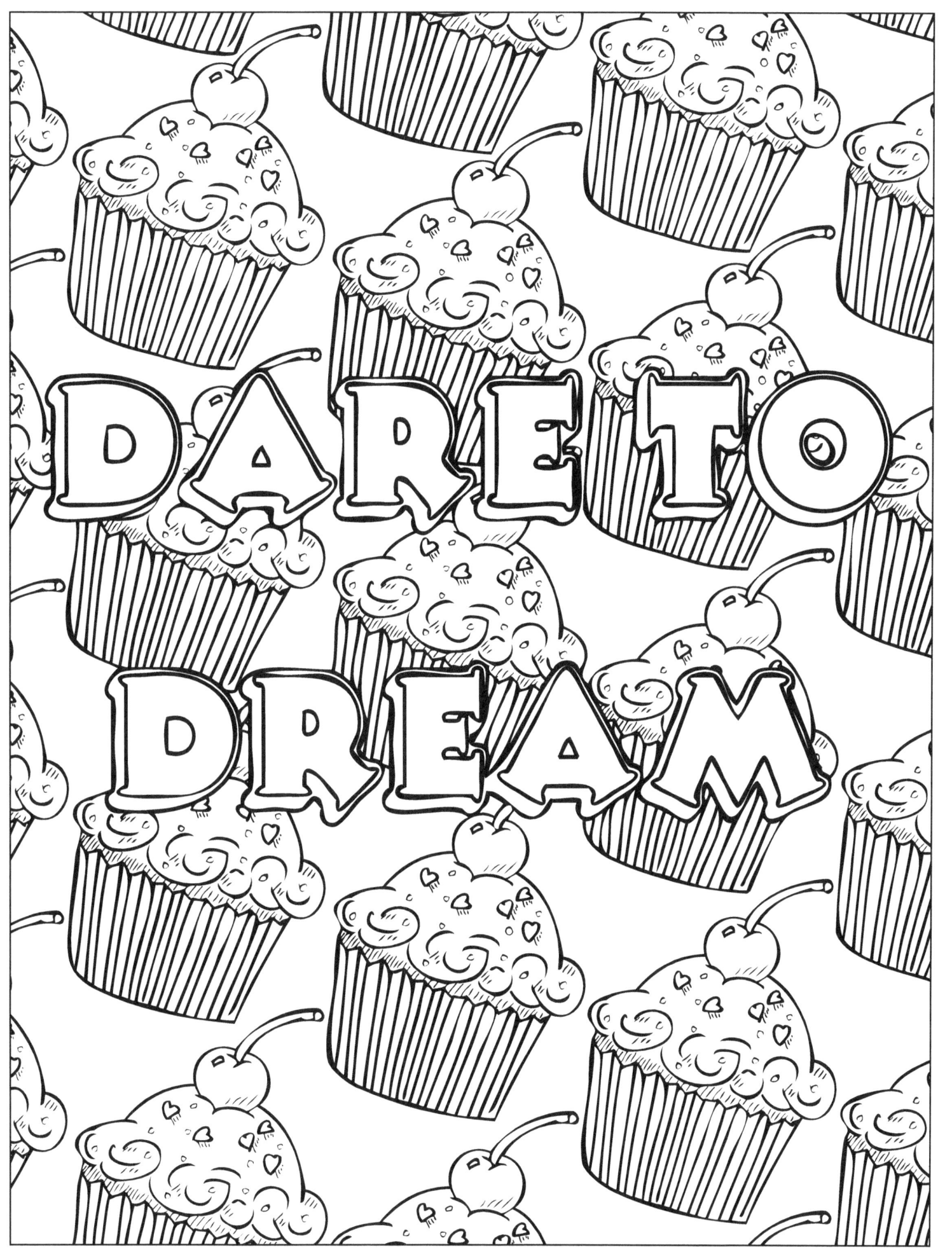

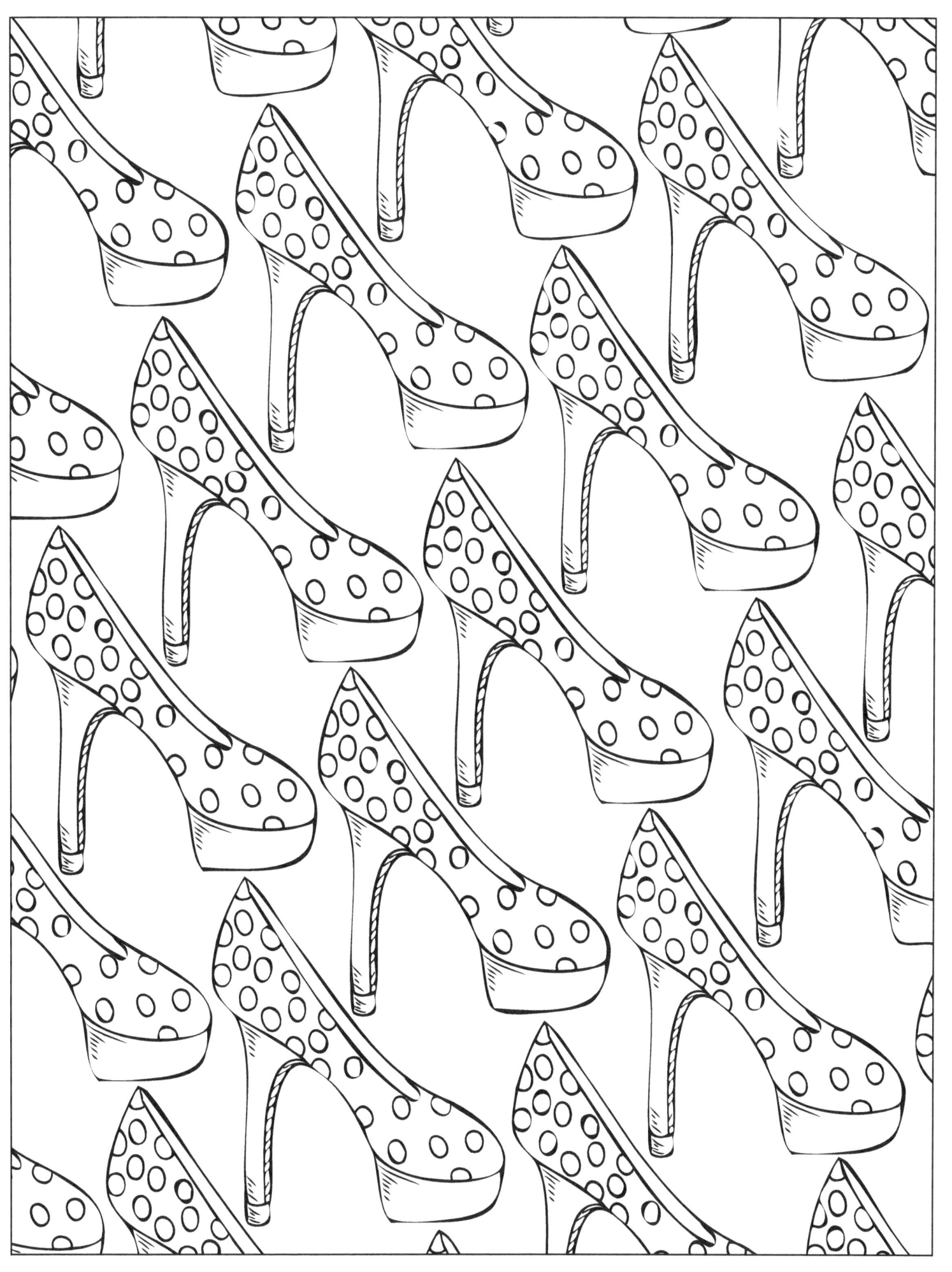

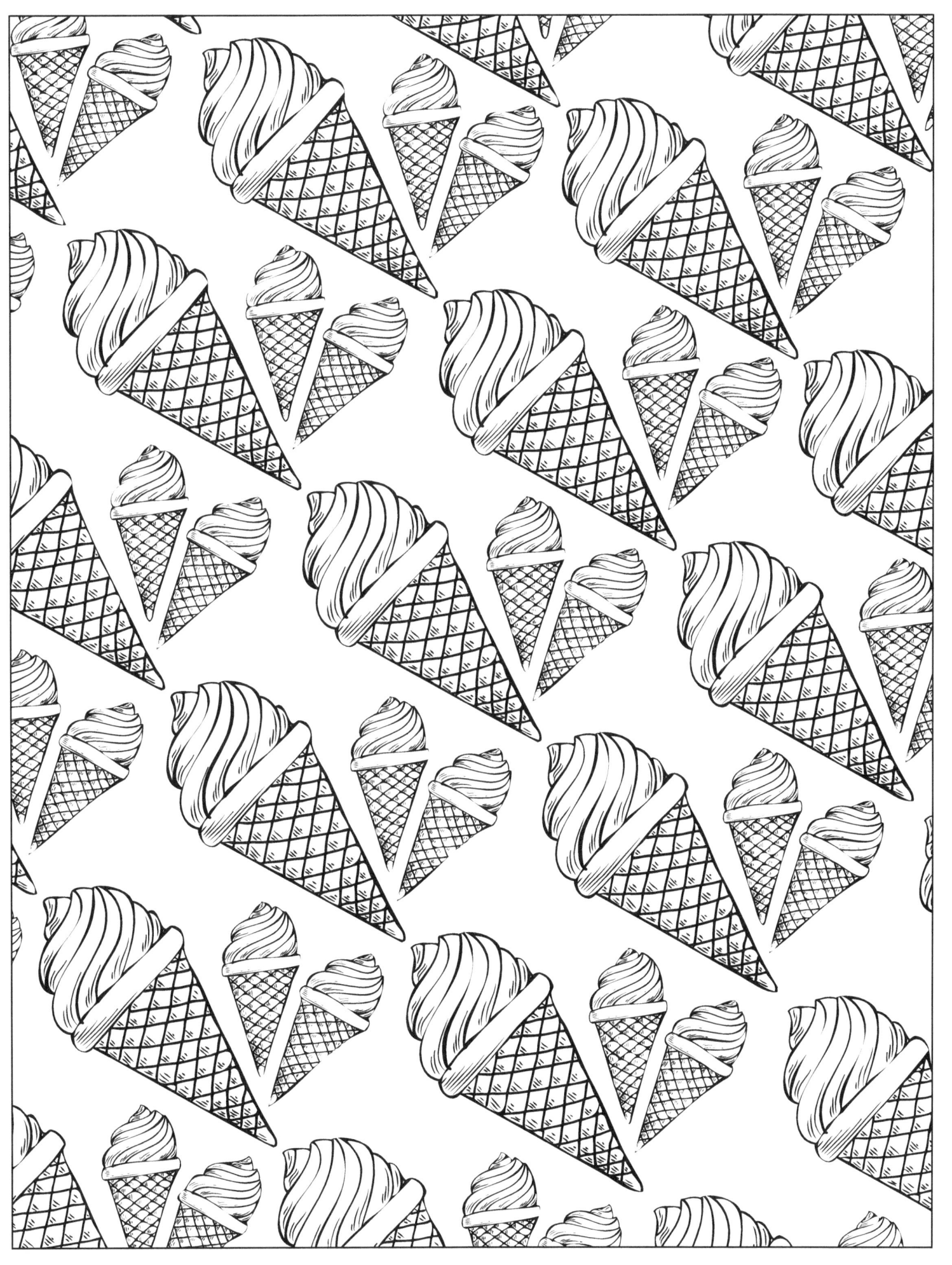

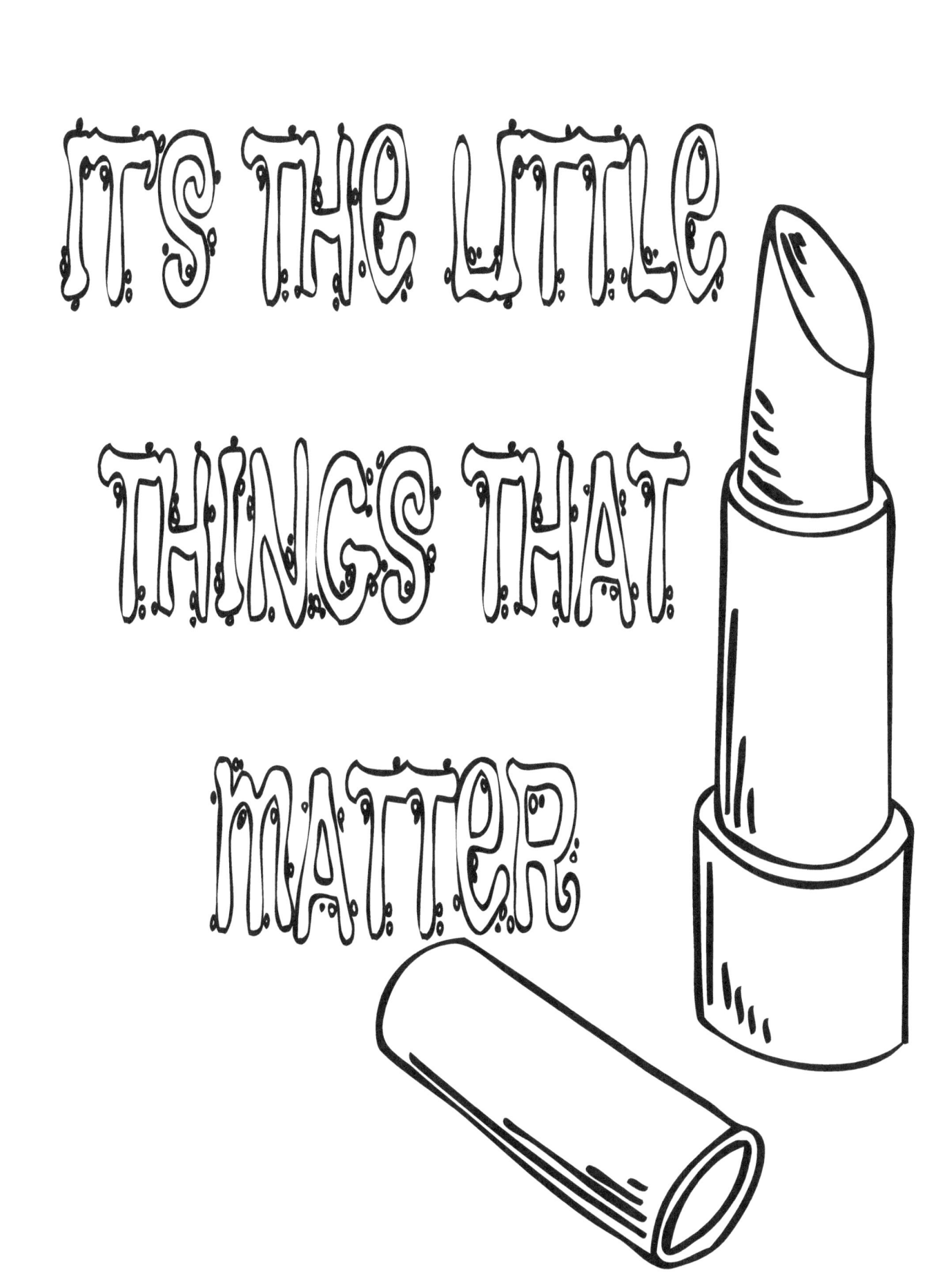

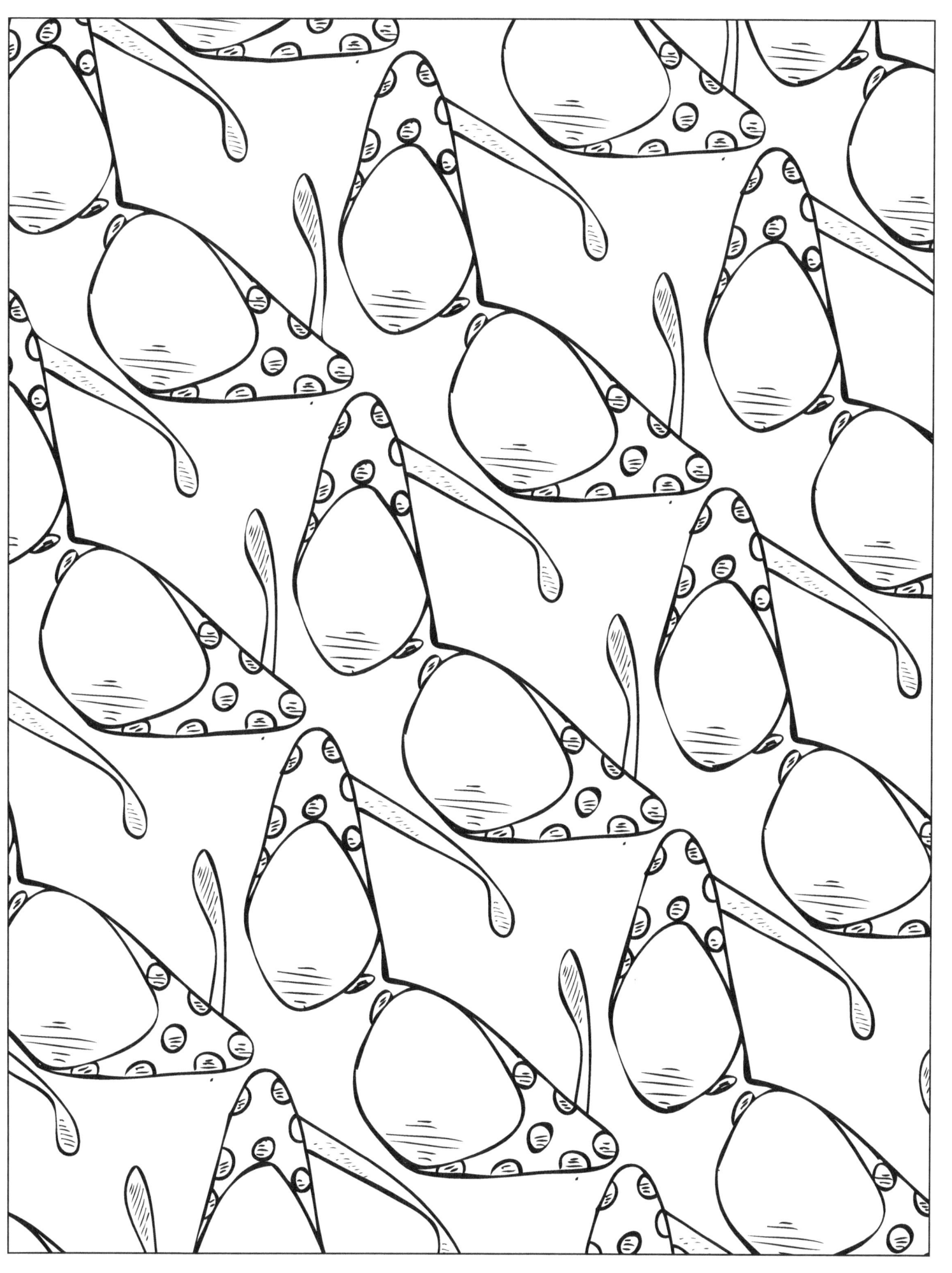

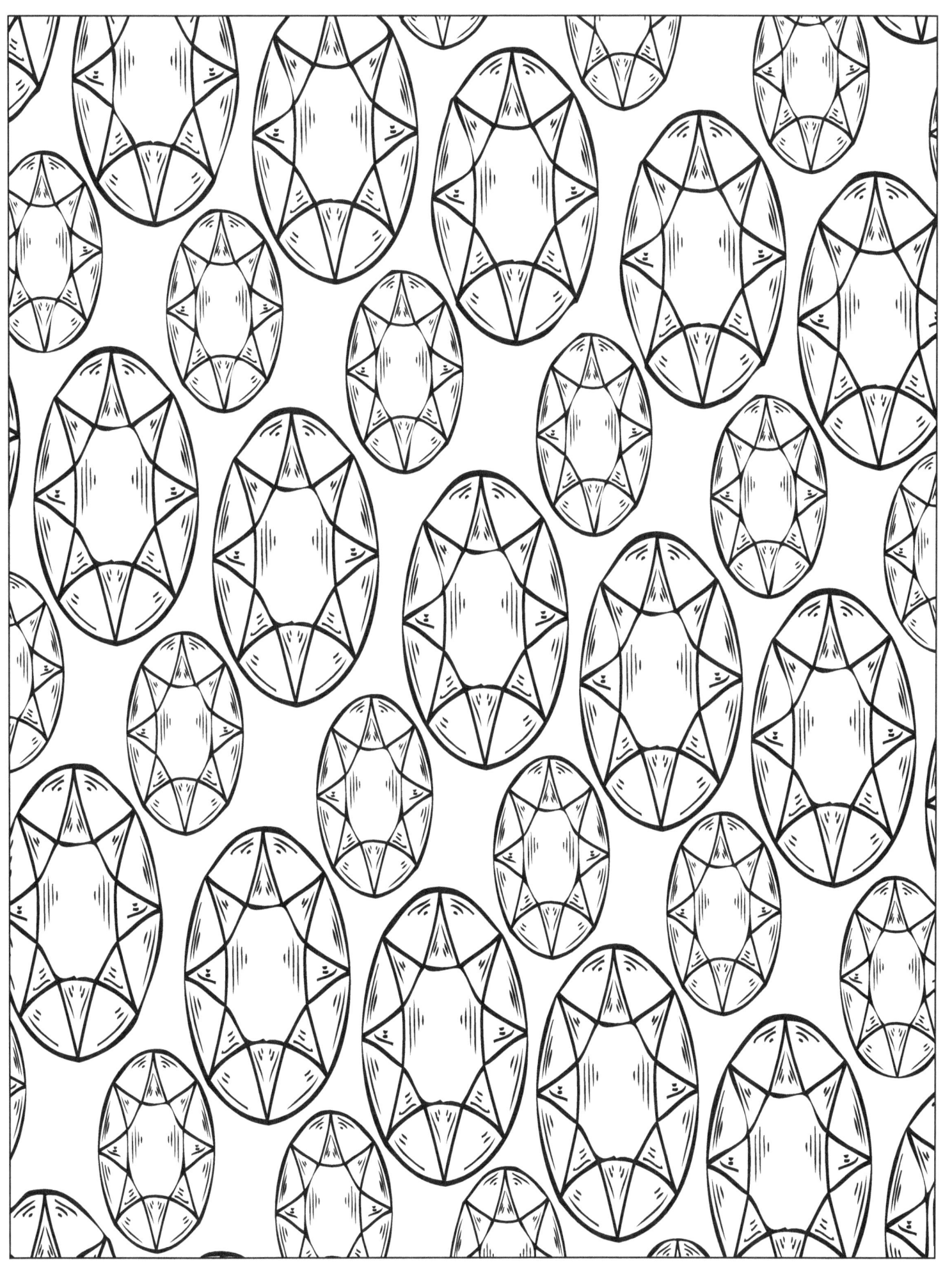

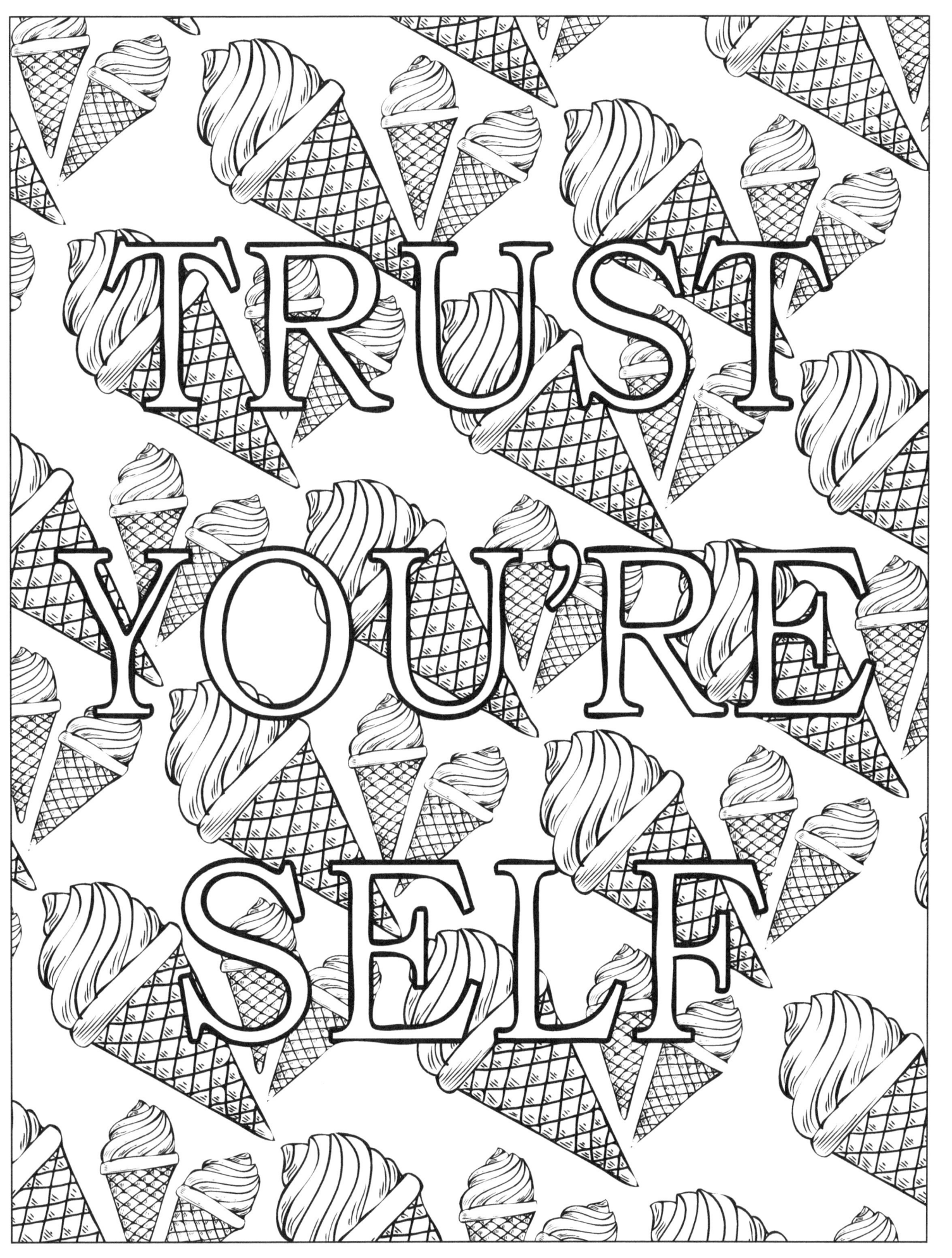

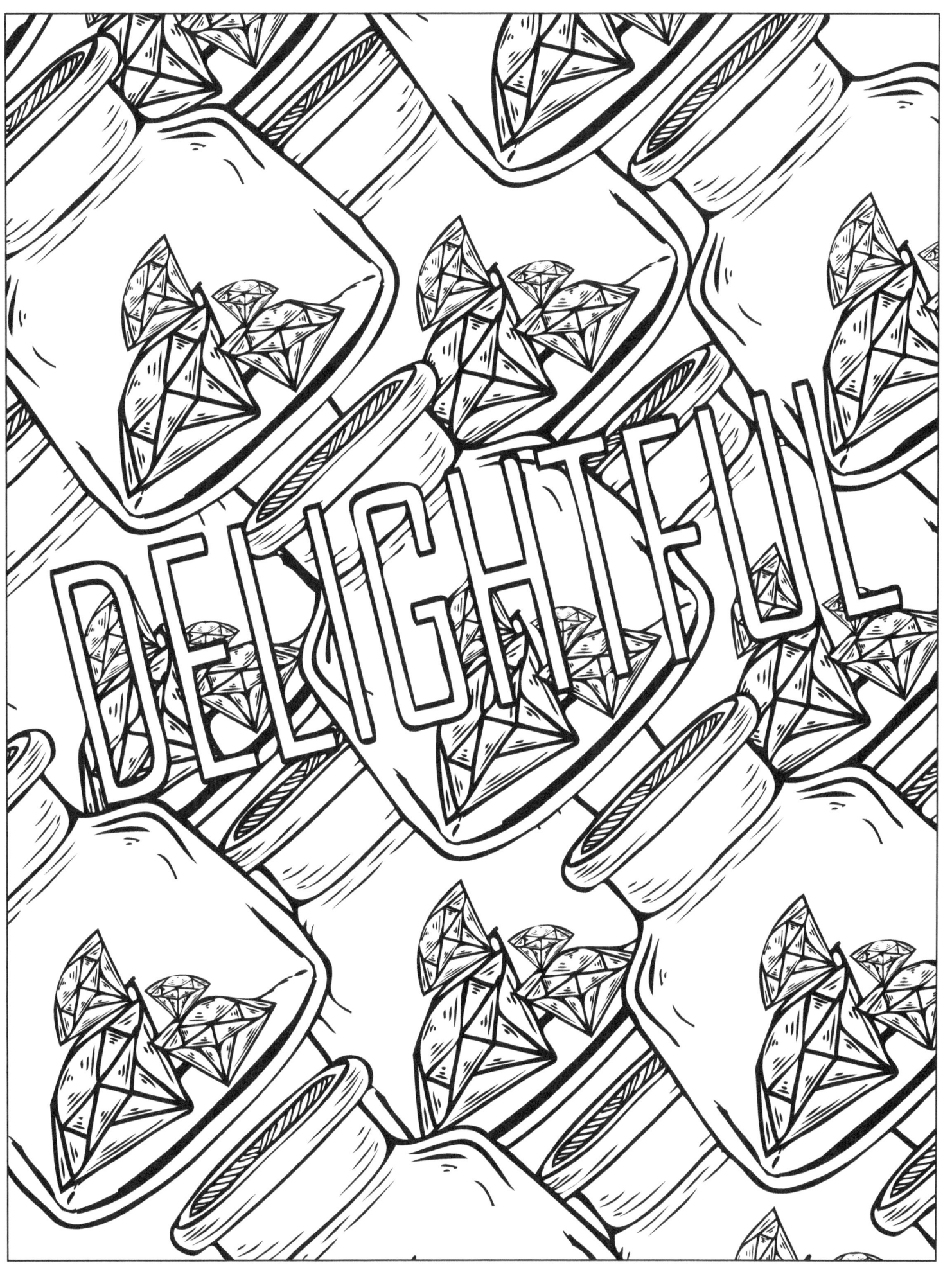

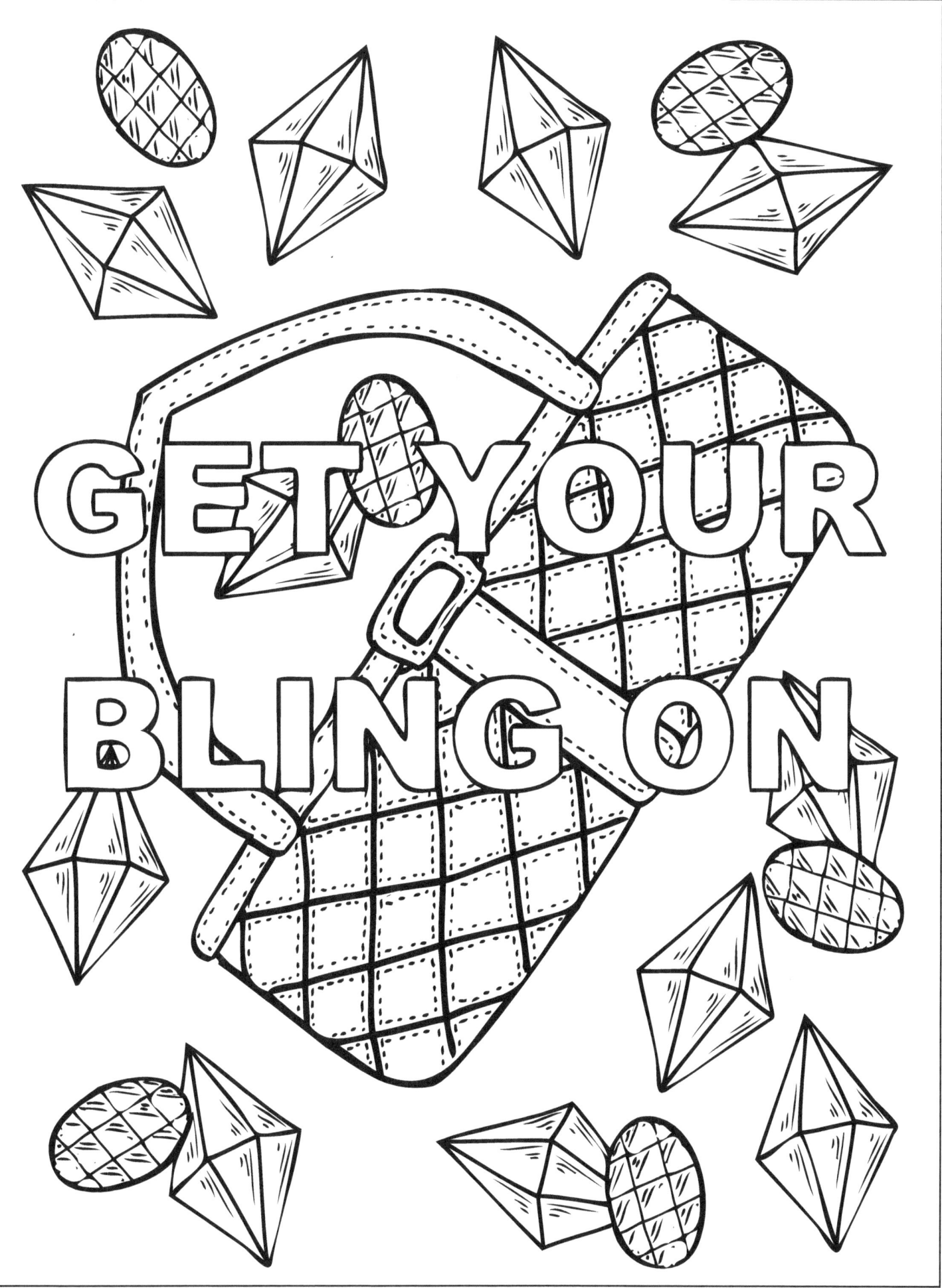

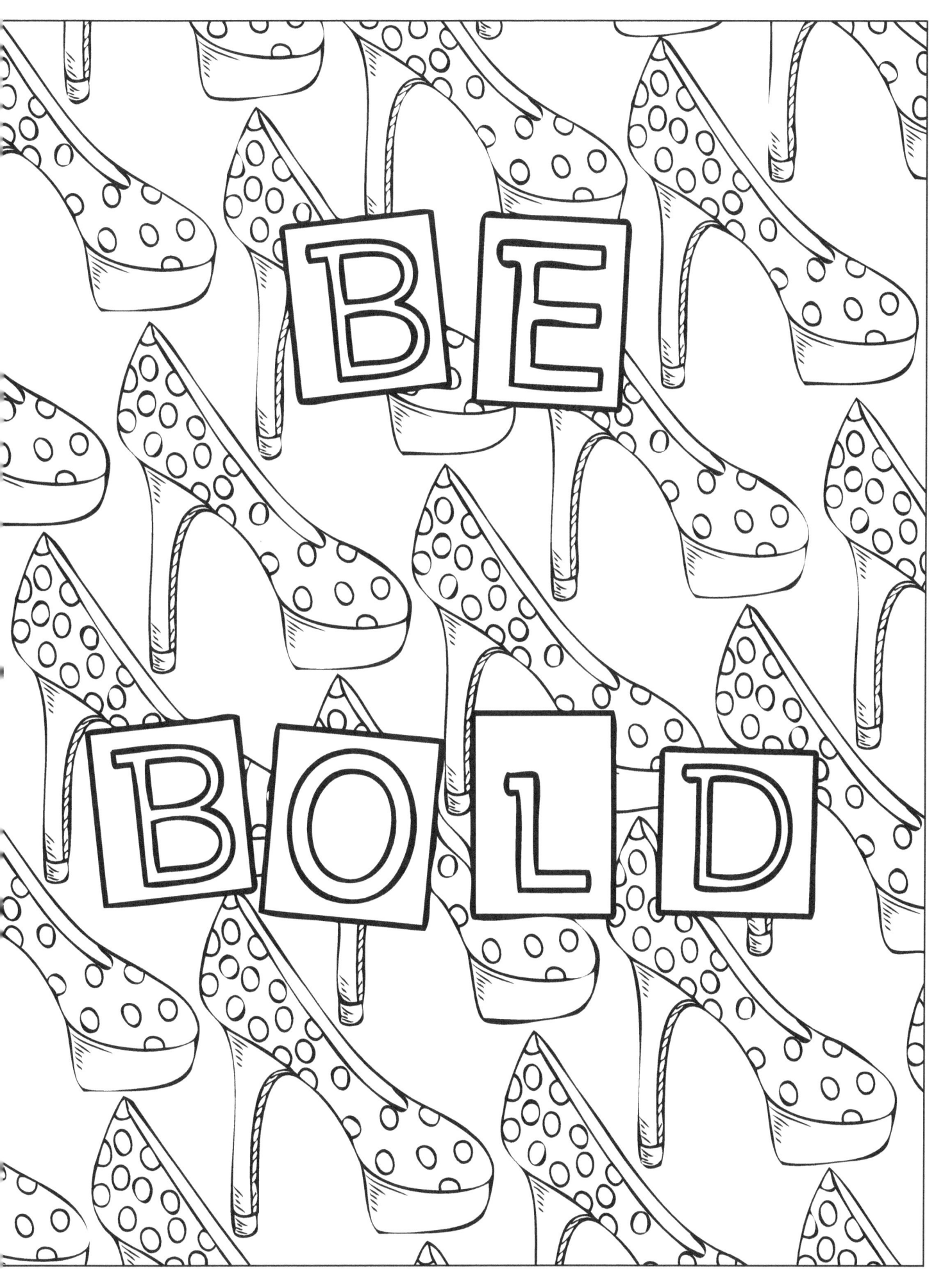

www.ingramcontent.com/pod-product-compliance
Lightning Source LLC
Chambersburg PA
CBHW082357220526
45470CB00008B/2773